365 WAYS TO LIVE GREEN

Diane Gow McDilda

Adamsmedia
avon, massachusetts

Published by
Adams Media, a division of F+W Media, Inc.
57 Littlefield Street, Avon, MA 02322. U.S.A.
www.adamsmedia.com

ISBN 10: 1-59869-808-7
ISBN 13: 978-1-59869-808-4

Printed in Canada.

J I H G F E

Library of Congress Cataloging-in-Publication Data
is available from the publisher.

This publication is designed to provide accurate and authoritative information with regard
to the subject matter covered. It is sold with the understanding that the publisher is
not engaged in rendering legal, accounting, or other professional advice. If legal advice
or other expert assistance is required, the services of a competent professional person
should be sought.

—From a *Declaration of Principles* jointly adopted by a Committee of the
American Bar Association and a Committee of Publishers and Associations

Many of the designations used by manufacturers and sellers to distinguish their product are claimed as trademarks. Where those designations appear in this book and Adams
Media was aware of a trademark claim, the designations have been printed with initial
capital letters.

Contains material adopted and abridged from *The Everything® Green Living Book*, by Diane
Gow McDilda, Copyright ©2007, F+W Publications, Inc.

This book is available at quantity discounts for bulk purchases.
For information, please call 1-800-289-0963.

CONTENTS

QUIZ: *How Big Is Your Eco-Footprint?*

So, just how "green" are you? Most people want to tread lightly on the planet, but they really aren't sure how big an impact they are making. If you are curious to see if you are a help or hindrance to the planet, take this quiz and find out. Just pick the answer that best suits your lifestyle.

THE QUESTIONS:

1	HOW OFTEN DO YOU RECYCLE?
A	I am a recycling nut. I recycle everything I can: paper, aluminum, printer cartridges, you name it.
B	I recycle when it's convenient as long as it doesn't require any excessive thought or effort on my part.
C	I don't have the time or the patience to recycle. I'm a busy person.

2	DO YOU USE RECYCLED PRODUCTS?
A	I try to reduce what I need, but when I do have to make purchases, I opt for recycled products whenever possible.
B	If I remember to look for the recycle triangle logo, I will usually buy that product.
C	So that's what they're doing with all the stuff other people recycle?

3	HOW MANY OF YOUR APPLIANCES HAVE THE ENERGY STAR LABEL?
A	Every single one of them that's available with the Energy Star label. I only buy products that are energy-efficient.
B	When I'm out shopping, I look for the Energy Star label. I try to purchase efficient appliances, but I won't sacrifice what I ultimately want.
C	I buy the appliances I want and need regardless of whether they're efficient. If there's an Energy Star label on one of my appliances, it's pure coincidence.

4	**HOW MUCH OF YOUR HOUSE IS MADE FROM SUSTAINABLE MATERIALS?**
A	My entire house is made of recycled or sustainable materials. In fact, it is LEED certified.
B	My house wasn't built using sustainable materials, but every time I renovate, I use sustainable and recycled materials.
C	I leave all the purchasing decisions to the builders. If they want to use sustainable or recycled materials, they can. It doesn't matter to me.

5	**DO YOU USE ANY FORM OF RENEWABLE ENERGY IN YOUR HOME?**
A	I purchase renewable energy from the local utility that's generated from landfill gas. Otherwise, I'd have a windmill or solar cells.
B	I'm evaluating different options. My local utility just started a renewable energy option. It costs a little more, but it's worth it. I'm also looking at adding solar cells to the house.
C	I think I heard something about the local utility using renewable energy, but I think it costs more, so I don't think I'll sign up for it.

6	**WHAT KIND OF GAS MILEAGE DOES YOUR CAR GET?**
A	I don't own a car.
B	Fifty miles to the gallon, baby!
C	I'm not really sure, but I'm guessing about fifteen.

7	**HOW OFTEN TO DO YOU ELIMINATE CAR TRIPS?**
A	I don't own a car. My primary means of transportation are my feet, my bike, and mass transit.
B	I try to eliminate at least one car trip a day by riding my bike or walking. I also try to carpool when car trips are really necessary.
C	My car is an extension of me. I wouldn't think of using any other kind of transportation.

8	**HOW OFTEN DO YOU EAT MEAT?**
A	I really don't eat meat. On rare occasions, I'll have a taste.
B	I eat it regularly, but I try to buy local meat raised organically.
C	I eat meat like Cookie Monster eats cookies.
9	**WHAT KIND OF SEAFOOD DO YOU EAT?**
A	I rarely eat seafood, but when I do, it's usually clams or mussels.
B	I eat seafood every couple of weeks, and it's usually shrimp that's been caught in the wild or farmed in the United States.
C	I love Atlantic halibut and flounder and eat it every chance I get.
10	**WHAT KIND OF PET DO YOU HAVE?**
A	I got my two dogs from the local animal shelter. I got my cat from a purebred rescue group.
B	My dog came from the animal shelter, but I really wanted a purebred cat with papers, so I bought it from a breeder.
C	I checked, but my local animal shelter didn't have Amazon parrots, so I went online. I had a boa constrictor, but it got big so I let it go.

SCORING:

For every **A** answer, give yourself 2 points.
For every **B** answer, give yourself 1 point.
For every **C** answer, give yourself 0 points.

HOW BIG IS YOUR FOOTPRINT?

20 to 15 points You have a petite and delicate footprint. Earth needs more inhabitants like you!

14 to 9 points Your footprint shows potential. Just a few more eco-friendly acts and you'll be reducing your shoe size.

8 to 0 points Your footprint rivals that of Sasquatch. You are hereby challenged to stop stomping around on the planet.

CHAPTER 1

The choices you can make . . .

IN YOUR THINKING

1 This Is Not a New Problem

The state of the environment has been a controversial topic for many years. There are disappearing flora and fauna, depleted stores of natural resources, rising temperatures worldwide—and many fingers pointing at who or what is to blame. Collective care and nurturing of the planet has waxed and waned over the decades, but today more people than ever seem to want to get involved and make changes in their lifestyles. So where do you start if you're looking to live a greener life? The truth is, there are plenty of places. The media coverage is extensive these days. It's practically impossible to listen to the radio, watch television, or read a newspaper without hearing about global climate change. The majority of scientists agree that action needs to be taken to stop, and eventually reverse, the trend of global warming.

2 The Greenhouse Effect—What's Really Going On

Agents causing global warming work collectively to increase the earth's temperature. Greenhouse gases—such as carbon dioxide, methane, nitrous oxide, and ground-level ozone—trap heat within the atmosphere, causing a warming effect similar to that in a greenhouse. Changes in land use have also impacted global climate change but not to the degree that greenhouse gases have. Clearing forestland for development increases the warming. Because trees absorb carbon dioxide and convert it to oxygen, cutting them down without replacing them means more carbon dioxide stays in the earth's atmosphere. The result is global warming and an increased potential for far-reaching consequences. Storms may become more severe, biodiversity may be adversely affected as ecosystems change, and polar icecaps may melt, causing ocean water levels to rise. Large-scale environmental impacts can increase potential dangers to public health.

3 The World Chooses to Work Together

No one person, no one country, no one continent is truly independent. World agencies recognize this fact and work together toward consensus on topics such as protecting sensitive coral reefs and diverse ocean populations, managing forests to allow logging while maintaining sustainable growth, ensuring air quality not just for individual communities but the world over, reducing the damaging effects of fossil fuel, and understanding the impacts of chemicals on people and the environment. However, individual efforts are essential to help improve all aspects of the environment. No one person is independent of other living things, and no one ecosystem is independent of the others.

4 The United Nations Calls for Action

In 1997, under the auspices of the United Nations, representatives met in Kyoto, Japan, to discuss global air quality. The result was the Kyoto Treaty, an international framework for managing greenhouse gases and improving air quality. The agreement binds nations to restrict their greenhouse gas emissions over time. Developed nations must submit to more stringent restrictions than developing nations. The goal is for each developed nation to release fewer greenhouse gases by 2012 than it did in 1990. The target emissions rates were negotiated on a country-by-country basis. Developing nations are exempt from reducing emissions until 2012. To date, more than 160 nations have ratified the treaty, including 35 developed nations. The United States and Australia have refrained from ratifying the treaty, claiming it would cost jobs and hurt their domestic economies.

5 The European Union Pulls Together

Countries in the European Union, in compliance with the Kyoto Treaty, limit the amount of carbon dioxide individual power plants and other

THE CHOICES YOU CAN MAKE . . . **IN YOUR THINKING**

large sources of emissions are allowed to produce within a certain time frame. Facilities whose emissions fall below the emissions cap can sell credits to facilities that overshoot their target emissions. The amount of carbon dioxide facilities are allowed to produce will be gradually reduced over time, resulting in fewer emissions. Because carbon dioxide is one of the principle culprits in global warming, carbon trading has been lauded as a way to offset emissions. In 2008, the European Union is expected to phase in regulations incorporating more industries and more greenhouse gases into the program.

Determine Your Impact

In the United States, some states are looking to renewable energy sources—wind, water, and solar energy—for electricity. To date, twenty-three states and the District of Columbia have set standards for how much of their electricity must be generated by renewable sources. Individuals can offset their own carbon production using a variety of measures. They can determine their impact on global warming by calculating the amount of carbon dioxide they produce. Calculations are based on size of household, miles driven and types of cars, air miles flown, and the amount of garbage generated. Web sites such as *www.conservationfund.org* assist people with the calculations.

Are We Risking Our Natural Resources?

The disappearance of natural resources damages an area and limits its viability to sustain a population. The population could be trees, sea grass, animals, or even people. Often, this damage is the result of beneficial activities performed irresponsibly. For example, wastewater discharged into an estuary can alter the salinity, affecting the lifecycle of sea grass and fish nurseries. If fishing is a source of income for a community, not only will improper treatment and disposal of wastewater damage natural resources, but it will harm the local economy as well.

8 The Push to Conserve and Change

On a larger scale, natural resources can be impacted to a point that they can no longer be repaired. Species cannot be brought back, and populations can no longer survive on the land. For example, damage from deforestation impacts biodiversity, causes soil erosion, and limits the farming of an area. However, all around the globe, people are gaining a better understanding that one system cannot operate at the expense of another. Conservation of natural resources has become a priority for businesses and governments, which tout sustainability as a way to strike a balance between helping the environment and preventing economic or personal hardship.

9 Sustainability Is a Choice

Sustainability is the balance between people and the environment. Air, water, and land are all impacted by the behavior and actions of human beings, but these impacts can be controlled so they do not cause as much damage while allowing all involved to maintain a comfortable existence. The art of sustainable living is the ability to support communities today without jeopardizing the environment for tomorrow. Maintaining sustainability isn't just up to corporations and governments, however; individuals bringing it into their everyday lives make an impact. Sustainability is making decisions with a new set of values—not a value set that hangs over your head like a cloud, but an understanding that there's a great deal you can do to preserve the environment for future generations while providing for yourself today.

10 Understand Traditional Energy Sources

The electrical power grid puts energy at your fingertips. Most electricity is generated from burning coal—a limited resource—and even with recent improvements in technology, it can be a detriment to the environment. Coal is a type of fossil fuel—the carbon-based power behind today's society. The name *fossil fuels* isn't an arbitrary choice. Formed about 300 million years ago, fossil fuels are made from plants and trees that died, fell into swamps and oceans, and were covered by more and more dead plants and trees. Eventually, sand and clay piled up and turned to rock, squeezing any remaining water out of the decayed plants and trees. After exposure to heat and pressure in the earth's crust over hundreds of millions of years, fossils turned into common fuels: coal, oil, and natural gas.

11 The Use of Fossil Fuels Is Changing Our World

Burning fossil fuels produces the energy necessary to run homes, offices, and automobiles. In the process, it releases pollutants and contributes to global warming. Two of those pollutants—sulfur dioxide and nitrogen oxide—react with water or moisture in the air to form nitric and sulfuric acids. These chemicals fall to the earth in the form of acid rain, damaging trees, soil, and waterways. Mercury that escapes coal-burning power plants through smoke stacks may wind up settling on rivers, lakes, estuaries, and bays. This mercury is dangerous, as you will learn later on in the chapter on what you should eat. Urban ozone, or smog, is also a by-product of coal-burning power plants. Smog can be detrimental to people, particularly children and the elderly, in whom it can cause wheezing, shortness of breath, and coughing. There are countless reasons why people have started to look at alternatives when it comes to providing electricity —these are only some of them.

12 The Solar Energy Option

Solar power converts energy from the sun into electricity. The two basic methods of using solar power to generate electricity are: concentrated solar power (CSP) plants and photovoltaic (PV) cells. The CSP plants are more mechanical in nature. Sunlight is used to heat a fluid, which then operates a generator and produces electricity. It operates much like a conventional power plant, but the energy source is sunlight rather than fossil fuels such as coal or natural gas. The PV uses sunlight to move electrons in a solar cell, which produces electricity. There are few mechanical or moving parts with this type of operation.

13 Is Solar Power Right for You?

Solar power is still slightly more expensive than traditional fossil fuel options, but the cost for solar power is expected to decrease as more private and public utility plants appear and solar cell technology advances. Many municipalities have installed solar power systems at locations with high-energy demands, such as schools and municipal administration buildings. Federal, state, and local organizations and governments fund incentives and rebate programs for homeowners who install residential solar units. These programs help offset the cost of installing home solar units. A variable sometimes left out of the economic calculation is that once a solar unit is paid for, the electricity is free.

14 What's Wind Power?

Today windmills are used to harness the wind's kinetic energy. Wind moves the mill's blades, which rotate a shaft that in turn moves gears connected to a generator. The generator creates electricity. Not only is wind renewable, it's clean, and it doesn't produce any deleterious by-products that other forms of energy do. Wind energy doesn't depend on process water as do coal and nuclear power. Wind power is generated domestically; there is no dependence on other countries to produce energy for local use. Also, harnessing wind power doesn't require mining operations as coal does, but there are some drawbacks to wind energy, including the negative impact of windmills on wild bird populations. Birds may be killed or injured if they fly into rotating windmill blades.

15 Biomass and Methane as Alternative Options

Biomass is a collective term that means producing energy from plants or animals. One common method is burning plant material to heat water and generate electricity. Feedstock for biomass power facilities generally includes agricultural waste left over from harvesting, energy crops grown specifically for use as biomass, forestry remains after timber harvesting, and wood left over from mill operations. Facilities can operate with either a pure biomass feedstock or with combined biomass and coal. The other common method of creating biomass includes digesting organic material like sludge or manure to produce methane, which is then burned, or flared, to produce electricity. Wastewater treatment plants are beginning to digest sludge at their facilities and then use the methane generated to help operate the treatment plants.

16 Get to Know the Geothermal Power

For every 100 meters you go below ground, the temperature of the rock increases about 3 degrees Celsius. Deep under the surface, water sometimes makes its way close to the hot rock and turns into boiling hot water or steam. Wells, some shallow and some miles deep, are drilled into the reservoirs and bring hot water or steam to the surface. Geothermal energy is most abundant and more easily accessible in places like Hawaii and Alaska where the geothermal reservoirs are closer to the surface. The shifting and moving tectonic plates in these areas enable the water heated from the magma below to escape more easily to the surface. Geothermal electricity is available virtually anywhere but is located much deeper, making retrieval less cost-effective. Geothermal energy is most heavily utilized in California and Nevada.

17 Harness Hydropower

Hydropower plants harness the kinetic energy of flowing water to power machinery or make electricity. There are typically three different types of hydropower facilities:

- Impoundment
- Diversion
- Pumped storage

The most common is impoundment in a dam that stores the water in a reservoir. Water flowing through the dam spins a turbine, which uses a generator to make electricity and sends it out to the grid. A diversion facility does not use a dam but instead diverts a portion of the river. Pumped storage requires the pumping of water from a lower reservoir to a higher reservoir so the water can be released when electrical demands are high.

18 Understand the Truth about Nuclear Power

Although a bane to many environmentalists, nuclear power is still considered a viable option when it comes to alternatives to coal-powered facilities. Nuclear power is usually created by splitting either a uranium or plutonium atom, but other radioactive elements can be used. The splitting releases an incredible amount of energy, which is

THE CHOICES YOU CAN MAKE . . . **IN YOUR THINKING**

used to heat water and drive a steam turbine. The power plants are usually very clean and safe when operated correctly. However, problems associated with nuclear power include the partial meltdown of a reactor at Three Mile Island near Middletown, Pennsylvania, in 1979 and the explosion and widespread radioactive contamination at the Chernobyl nuclear power plant in the former Soviet Union in 1986.

THE CHOICES YOU CAN MAKE . . . **IN YOUR THINKING**

CHAPTER 2

The choices you can make . . .

WHEN IN YOUR HOME AND YARD

19 Change the Way You Clean

When picking out cleansers for the home, try to avoid unnecessary dyes and fragrances and avoid extra packaging. Be careful with concentrates. Using a cleanser that comes in concentrated form does save on packaging by allowing consumers to mix it up and dilute it at home. But in its concentrated form care must be taken to avoid exposure to people and the environment from the highly concentrated ingredients. People cleaned their houses long before all the fancy products hit the market and the commercials hit the airways. They used common ingredients, a little know how, and mixing and managed to get the dirt and dust up. A lot of times these cleaning ingredients are less expensive than the new and improved products being advertised.

20 Use Products Smarter

Here's a list of more natural and less toxic cleaning ingredients and their uses:

- Vinegar can be mixed with water to clean floors.
- Borax mixed with lemon juice can be used to clean toilets.
- Lemon juice mixed with olive oil is great for polishing furniture.
- Use rubbing alcohol mixed with vinegar and water to clean your windows.
- Baking soda can be used to scrub stainless steel, iron, or copper pots. Be sure not to use it on aluminum pots.

21 Kill Pests, Not the Environment

No one wants to see roaches scurrying or ants marching across their kitchen counters or down their walls. But before using pesticides, people can consider other alternatives available to control pests. One of the first steps to reducing pests and insects in the house is

removing whatever it is that they are attracted to. Keep counters and floors clean of food scraps. And dripping faucets and soaking dishes should be avoided because they serve as a water source enticing insects into the kitchen. Keep foods that pests find attractive such as flour, macaroni, and cornmeal in the refrigerator to eliminate easy access by bugs.

22 Use Natural Remedies for Pesky Pests

Here is a list of natural ways to rid your home of some of the more common pests without using pesticides:

- Follow a trail of ants to find where they are coming in. Sprinkle chili pepper, dried peppermint, or borax to steer them away.
- For cockroaches mix borax, sugar, and flour and sprinkle it in the infested area. Also try sprinkling borax behind light switches, under sinks, and in the back of cabinets to kill roaches.
- Feeding a dog or cat brewer's yeast mixed in with their food is said to deter fleas.
- Look to cedar chips to drive off moths.
- If there is a problem with rodents, consider getting a cat. If that does not work, traps may be the best bet. Humane traps are available that allow catch and release of varmints.
- Keep pantries free of moths and other pests with insect traps.
- Diligent vacuuming can eliminate dust mites. If dust mites are in bedding, wash it regularly and cover pillows and mattresses in mite-free pillow and mattress cases.

23 Use Your Dishwasher

There is no need to guess or speculate, there is actually scientific data to prove which method of washing dishes is more efficient. Researchers at the University of Bonn in Germany determined that using a dishwasher cleaned the dishes better and saved energy and time.

24 Get the Most Out of Your Washing Water

For someone who's a diehard for washing dishes by hand, or if you do not have a dishwasher, the folks in Bonn have recommendations for getting the most out of washing:

- Remove large pieces of food left on the dishes.
- Don't rinse any of the dishes before washing. This goes if someone is using an automatic dishwasher too.
- Use two sinks: one with hot soapy water to wash and one filled with cooler water to rinse.
- Do not go overboard with soap or detergent. Use only what's needed. It will conserve cleanser and won't over-suds the rinse water.

25 Think Outside the Box When Washing Clothes

There are a few ways to reduce impacts on the environment when doing the laundry. Washing clothes in cold water saves energy and colors. Using the smallest amount of soap or detergent will save money and natural resources.

26 Dry Smarter

Clotheslines aren't just for grandmothers in Arizona. There's no denying that using the sun to dry clothes saves energy. But clotheslines are rare these days. So if you aren't ready to quit using your dryer cold turkey, you may just want to cut back a little. When you do use your dryer, there are some steps that can be taken to make it more efficient. You shouldn't over dry clothes; take them out as they are dry. Don't overload the dryer and dry similar items together. Dryer sheets release chemicals as they bounce around in the dryer making clothes soft and reducing static electricity. These chemicals and fragrances can cause skin irritation or concern. Instead use chemical-free products that treat static electricity and soften clothes and can be used over and over again.

27 Consider Different Grass Options

Homeowners can decide how much time, effort, and expense they want to put into yard work, spending time and money mowing, applying fertilizers and pesticides. You can plant your lawn with a mixture of native tall grasses or plants that require little maintenance. Prairie grasses and flowers will grow taller than standard lawn grass and will decorate the yard with colorful flowers during different times of the year. Other plants and flowers can be added offering decorative alternatives to grass and giving lawns a less-manicured and wilder look. Short growing plants and ground cover can provide an alternative to standard grass while allowing people to walk on and play in the yard. The right grass substitute or no-mow lawn can mean reducing and possibly even eliminating the need to mow and fertilize all together.

28 Make Your Yard More Than a Yard

Multiple companies offer seed mixes of wildflowers and short grasses that can be thrown in the yard. These mixtures include ingredients such as ryegrass, clover, daisies, lavender, and thyme. You can make mixtures of ingredients according to geographical location, watering and lighting requirements, soil conditions, and mowing needs. Grasses grow at varying rates with some requiring more mowing than others, while others require no mowing at all. Ask your local florist or garden center for products or look some up online.

29 Look into the Drought-Resistant Yard

In the southern and southwestern United States, xeriscape landscaping has become a popular alternative to high-maintenance yards. Xeriscaping uses plants specifically selected for their drought-resistant qualities. In areas where water restrictions are common, these types of plants offer a pleasant alternative to standard lawns. One example is the use of clover instead of grass. Not only is clover drought-resistant, it's tolerant to weeds and insects, requires minimal mowing, and offers a soft cushion for walking.

30 Don't Update Your Mower; Use the Old One!

Either by personal choice or neighborhood covenants many people have lawns of green grass that need to be maintained. That's where choosing the right mower comes in. Anyone who wants to skip a trip to the gym should consider mowing his or her yard using a reel lawn mower. Reel mowers are the oldest of residential lawnmowers. The blades are attached to the wheels, and as the mower is manually pushed, the wheels roll, and the blades rotate cutting the grass. While some may choose this type of mower for nostalgia, others may opt for the simplicity. There is no engine or ignition to keep in working order and no fuel mixture to carefully store in the garage. Beyond not being dependent on fuel, reel lawn mowers don't produce any emissions.

31 Understand Electric Mowers

Electric lawnmowers are available that work well for small yards and gardens. While electric mowers do rely on electricity for power, they produce no emissions on site though the power plants where the electricity demand is realized do release emissions. Not only are they friendly for air quality, they're quiet and do not produce pollution either. Some can be equipped with grass catchers and even have mulch capabilities. Electric mowers are lightweight, and the handles can be folded for easy storage. Cordless mowers can be charged overnight to provide up to forty minutes of mowing time the next day.

32 Consider the Impact of Modern Mowing Machines

Newer power-driven lawnmowers are more efficient than older models, but they can still be produce smog-forming chemicals and carbon monoxide. Lawnmowers do not have catalytic converters, which are required on automobiles. These treat the exhaust before it escapes, removing nitrogen oxides, volatile organic compounds, and hydrocarbons before they can combine with sunlight to form smog. The EPA is currently working on legislation that would require the installation of catalytic converters in lawnmowers. But until then, why not get rid of that thing and use an old-fashioned one— it's safer!

33 Deal with the Clippings the Right Way

The Environmental Protection Agency (EPA) estimates that up to 31 million tons of yard waste is collected, transported, and processed by municipalities every year. Leaves and grass clippings need not be taken to the curb. They can be used in compost and made into mulch or used by themselves in planting beds and gardens. Keeping yard trimmings at home for use in the garden reduces waste processing and the need for transportation. If raking isn't your ideal past time, there are manual leaf sweepers available. You can use lawn sweepers to collect leaves from yards, sidewalks, and driveways, making them ready to put in the compost pile (*www.composters.com*).

34 Compost with Care

One way to pump up plants and get rid of garbage at the same time is to compost. Compost is made of recycled food scraps, yard trimmings, clean paper, and even fireplace ashes. Don't include meat, pet droppings, or oil and grease though because they can attract rodents that can carry disease and can kill the beneficial organisms. You can buy a compost unit from lawn and garden centers, online carriers, or even through local extension or utility offices. Or you can make one at home using materials such as chicken wire, bricks, or buckets. The organic material in the compost bin needs to be turned and watered regularly to mix up the contents from the inner portions of the pile to the outer portions. The material in the center of the pile decays as it is kept warm and moist, a perfect atmosphere for degradation. When the mixture turns into a dark brown, crumbly material that smells like earth it's ready to go. Using compost is a great way to improve soil texture and keep weeds from growing, it increases air and water absorption in the soil, and can be used as mulch in the lawn or garden. Compost makes great potting soil.

35 Use Native Plants; They're Less Needy

Using native plants when landscaping makes maintaining a healthy lawn even easier. Native plants are adapted to local climates and conditions so they don't need a lot of care to thrive. They have been flourishing for years without any help from humans. Native plants are accustomed to local pests so they do not depend on pesticides. Native plants are also acclimated to local weather conditions and rainfall meaning they don't need excessive watering or protection. Local birds and butterflies are often attracted to native species, making a yard a haven to animals. And native plants will live longer than exotics, saving time and money, and conserving natural resources too. Ultimately using native plants will cut down on the effort and energy needed to maintain a beautiful lawn.

36 Attract Beneficial Insects and Animals

Beneficial insects and animals can be very, well beneficial, when it comes to getting rid of pests in your garden. Ladybugs, lacewings, and ground beetles feed on aphids, cinch bugs, and weevils. Lizards, birds, and frogs will likely make a meal out of pesky caterpillars and grubs. But beneficials will not be attracted by the pests alone and sometimes need to be enticed with plants. Adding bordering flowers will attract beneficial insects by providing shelter and nectar. Not only will there be fewer pests, the beneficial bugs will help pollinate flowers, fruits, and vegetables. While beneficials are helpful, when it comes to countering an invasion in the garden, you may need a more hands-on approach to get rid of pests. Caterpillars, worms, and beetles can be hand picked and destroyed. Also mixing a few tablespoons of a strong smelling ingredient, such as cayenne, garlic, or horseradish with a quart of water and spraying it on plants can drive away some pests. Recipes for mildew and fungi treatments include common kitchen ingredients like baking soda and vinegar—do an online search to find these.

37 Beware of and Be Smart with Pesticides

The impacts of many synthetic pesticides are still unknown because many of the effects are long-term. The overuse of pesticides has been acknowledged, and proper application has been taken more seriously by individuals, corporations, and municipalities. People have begun to appreciate chemicals' destructive power and are using more safety precautions and following directions more closely. The EPA registers pesticides for use on the basis that they do not pose

THE CHOICES YOU CAN MAKE . . . **WHEN IN YOUR HOME AND YARD** unreasonable risks to people or the environment. Unfortunately, the long-term and synergistic effects are not always known when the chemicals are registered. By following the rules for a smart home and yard that are listed here, you should not have to use many pesticides. But if you do, be smart about it and research what you're doing to your lawn, family, and world before you spray chemicals into the air.

CHAPTER 3

The choices you can make . . .

WHEN CHOOSING WHERE TO BUILD

38 Choose the Right Location

If you are looking to relocate or build a house, you can take into account different locations and attributes that might make the change more environmentally friendly. With a public upsurge in environmental concerns, many cities and states have taken the initiative to make improvements and make themselves havens for environmentally friendly citizens. If you know where you are going to live, you can choose to use more environmentally friendly home designs and construction materials.

39 Get to Know the Green Cities and States

Many mayors are taking actions to improve air quality, reduce electrical use and production, encourage green building construction, allocate more green space, support nontraditional transportation, and set aside or improve areas for recreational activities. The U.S. Conference of Mayors is just one coalition working to improve cities in a variety of ways. In an effort to improve air quality, 238 cities have pledged accordance with the Climate Protection Agreement, a pact that encourages each city to reduce greenhouse gas emissions by 7 percent from 1990 levels by the year 2012. The organization shares ideas and outcomes from programs they have implemented, providing a network of environmental actions and results for others to learn from. This is just one example of communities working together to improve conditions in their own cities and towns.

40 Consider These Best Places to Live

When it comes to good stewardship, Austin, Texas; San Francisco, California; Portland, Oregon; Boulder, Colorado; and Seattle, Washington have been identified by organizations such as the Green Guide as showing success. Eugene, Oregon, got the top spot in the Green Guide's list for 2006 because of its numerous bike trails, open space, and commitment to renewable resources. Eighty-five percent of the city's power is provided by hydroelectricity and wind power. Chicago, Minneapolis, and Honolulu are very conscientious when it comes to encouraging clean air and water, promoting green building, and ensuring parks and open spaces are protected.

41 Don't Discount the Second-Tier States

States may not be involved on the same level as cities, but they still take measures to make themselves more environmentally friendly to homeowners. States on both coasts have come together to reduce greenhouse gas emissions. The West Coast Governors' Global Warming Initiative, including California, Oregon, and Washington, puts limits on greenhouse gas emissions and commits the states to using increasing amounts of renewable energy. Nine states—Connecticut, Delaware, Maine, Massachusetts, New Hampshire, New Jersey, New York, Rhode Island, and Vermont—formed the Regional Greenhouse Gas Initiative with similar aims to reduce greenhouse gas emissions.

42 Explore the Energy Star Label States

In fifteen states more than 20 percent of the homes have qualified for the Energy Star label. Energy Star criteria were created by the EPA and the Department of Energy to give homeowners and contractors' guidelines and direction when looking for more sustainable approaches to construction. Energy Star rates homes, businesses, and household products for energy efficiency. The Energy Star Web site, *www.energystar.gov*, has more information. Take a look and see if your house, office, or state qualifies!

43 Make an Informed Decision

If you are looking for a clean start in a new city, there are a few factors to consider when it comes to making a choice. Air quality is an important consideration when it comes to calling a place home. How does a city rank for fuel exhaust pollution? The EPA maintains an Air Quality Index (*www.airnow.gov*) that scores ozone and particulate matter for different cities across the United States. If you are looking for an official list, review *The Green Guide* Top 10 Green Cities, which is put out annually by the Green Guide Institute, an independent research organization that provides information for consumers so they can make informed environmental choices in their daily lives. Check out their Web site and the list at *www.thegreenguide.com*.

44 Know a Conscientious City When You See One

Another link to air quality is a city's ability to encourage environmentally friendly transportation. Mass transit systems cut down on the vehicles on the road, reduce parking and congestion problems, and limit or decrease greenhouse gas emissions and smog. Conscientious cities also provide carpool lanes, dedicated bicycle lanes, walking trails, and sidewalks and are designed to run efficiently without the need for individually owned vehicles. Look for cities that already use or are making headway with alternative fuels such as biomass, geothermal, hydroelectric, solar, and wind. Search Web sites for information on cities that use alternative fuels, such as *www.sustainlane.us* and *www.eere.energy.gov/greenpower*.

45 Look for Green Spaces within Cities

City designers that take into account not just buildings but green space understand an important aspect of improving environmental quality. Green spaces provided by a municipality include athletic fields and parks, walking and biking trails, and recreational water and clean water resources. The U.S. Green Building Council (USGBC) runs the Leadership in Energy and Environmental Design (LEED) program, setting criteria for what is considered a green building. LEED takes into account human and environmental health, sustainable site development, water savings, energy efficiency, material selection, and indoor environmental quality. Some builders specifically design houses or developments with sustainability in mind. When looking for a house, find out if the community includes any of these developments.

46. Rank the Town's Recycling Habits

Municipal recycling programs are another indication of a city's dedication to the environment. Recycling conserves natural resources, and it reduces the energy needed to make recycled products. If you're moving, consider choosing a city that encourages recycling with curbside programs and recycling centers that go beyond the standard glass, paper, and aluminum. Recycling programs offset the cost of waste disposal, and they also can generate income.

47. Investigate Your Water Worries

Feeling safe about the water delivered from the tap is something to consider, too. The EPA requires that municipalities' water quality be documented and reported as part of the Safe Drinking Water Act. The EPA does not maintain the data in a searchable format, but it can direct you to information on a particular water system. Towns, cities, and utilities should have this information on hand and may even post it on their Web sites. Drinking water should not contain compounds that are required to be monitored at levels exceeding the Drinking Water Standards. Data that is available for review should note any levels in excess of allowable concentrations.

48. Think about Your New Life in the Town

Even if you already know what town or city you are going to live in, you still need to choose which part of town to live in. If you know where you'll be working, that's a start. Then you can consider all of your commutes—to work, school, the grocery store, and other regular activities. Take into account the frequency of those trips and when they'll be made. Choose the location that minimizes your driving time. What appears to be a great location at two in the afternoon may turn ugly during rush hour. If living close to work or school just isn't an option, look at mass transit routes and other transportation opportunities. Is carpooling an option? Or is a subway or train station located nearby? An activity that a family member participates in regularly may also be a controlling consideration. Weigh all the factors.

49 Be a Part of a Town that Pushes for Green

A number of larger cities have encouraged the construction of green homes within the city limits to avoid or at least control urban sprawl. Although sprawl may be the bane of society, suburbs can be designed in ways that reduce their potential impact on the environment and conserve natural resources and wildlife habitat. Cities are choosing to develop more efficiently in the suburbs with mixed-use neighborhoods that are bicycle and pedestrian friendly. The aim is that although people may have to drive to work, they should be able to walk or bike about easily once they get home.

50 Understand Urban Sprawl

Although debated by many, urban sprawl is blamed for much of society's woes. Urban sprawl fragments and destroys wildlife habitat and corridors. The persistent construction of low-density housing requires additional roads and cars to navigate them. Unless houses or developments are constructed to be independent from municipal services, other infrastructure systems such as water, wastewater, and electricity have to be expanded to accommodate spreading cities.

51   Use Your Natural Habitat to Warm/Cool Your House

If the location is set and all that's left is to build, a variety of design considerations cam make a dream home a little greener. First off, let Mother Nature help with heating and cooling. Take a good hard look at the plot you've chosen. In locations with warm climates, the broad side of the house should face north or south to avoid a direct hit—and resulting heat gain—from the sun. Deep overhangs will also help block the sun and reduce excessive heat gains by putting the house in the shade. Apply tint to windows, particularly sliding glass doors and large picture windows that can heat up a room quickly and force an air conditioner to work overtime. In colder climates, take advantage of the sun's heating abilities. Heat provided from the sun can be stored in the concrete or stone walls of a house, helping to keep it warm even after the sun goes down.

52   Enlist Nature-Made Solar Protection

Of course, there's always the completely organic solution for shading your house—planting a tree. Trees provide nature-made solar protection. Some trees are particularly useful in blocking the sun because of their height and shape. Some trees grow faster than others, so if time is of the essence when it comes to creating shade, plant a quicker-growing tree. It's important to choose a tree that is native to the location for optimal health and lower maintenance. If it's an option, retain as many of the existing trees as possible when building on a new lot. They'll provide shade and have already proven themselves as being viable on the property.

53   Insulate from the Ground Up

Soil can also be an essential source for maintaining the temperature of a home. By building a home partially below grade, you can maintain a more moderate temperature year-round. The earth is usually

THE CHOICES YOU CAN MAKE . . . **WHEN CHOOSING WHERE TO BUILD** cooler than above ground, so heating may be necessary to maintain a comfortable temperature in cold weather. However, because the soil provides insulation, the heat will remain in the house.

54 Get Some Serious Help

When considering the design of a green home, you can work with contractors and architects who are energy conscious and will help you to achieve your goals. The LEED program tries to educate architects, contractors, and engineers on designing and constructing more energy-efficient and environmentally friendly buildings, but it does not have a certification course specifically geared toward private homes. Some extension programs work with local builders and designers, providing classes and information in this area.

55 Remodel and Recycle

You may be interested in renovating an existing home to make it greener. Many of the same new construction considerations apply to renovation. You should be able to discuss alternatives with your contractor to ensure that sustainable elements are brought into the design. Also, if you are demolishing older portions of a home, the material being removed should be reused or handled properly to avoid excessive waste. If your contractor is not familiar with recycling programs in the area, make some phone calls. Habitat for Humanity, a nonprofit organization that builds homes, runs a program called ReStores that accepts donations of used or excess building materials in good condition. Local solid-waste authorities may have information on specific recyclers in the area. Try calling salvage companies as well.

CHAPTER 4

The choices you can make ...

WHEN CHOOSING HOW TO BUILD

56 Use the Right Construction Materials

Choosing building materials to preserve natural resources means using elements from renewable resources that help conserve energy and improve the health and well-being of those inside. Qualities to look for in these materials include conserving resources, improving indoor air quality, being energy efficient, and conserving water. Most important, make sure the materials are affordable not just to use for construction but also to operate on a month-by-month basis.

57 Make the Most of Recycled Materials

From the outside in, there are a variety of recycled materials available for building homes. Products made from recycled materials require less energy to produce and use ingredients that would otherwise need to be disposed of in a landfill or incinerator. Starting from the bottom up, the foundation of most homes can be made using concrete that incorporates fly ash (the remnants from coal power plants) and even recycled concrete. Depending on the construction, it could be possible to incorporate the foundation into the finished floor design, which would require fewer building materials than usual.

58 Try to Avoid Concrete

Concrete requires the mining of materials such as limestone, which alters the land and surface-water flow and affects inhabitants significantly. Its production is energy intensive, not just in mining and transport but in processing as well; this energy is usually produced by coal-fired power plants. Carbon dioxide is produced by the power plants used to supply electricity to the processing facility and as part of the chemical process of converting limestone into lime. The process also produces sulfur dioxide and nitrous oxides. Particulate matter, or dust, is also created during the mining, storage, and transportation of the materials. Although the mining and processing associated with making concrete has improved over the decades, there are still issues that make reducing the amount produced practical and in our best interests.

59 Explore the Uses of Papercrete

Recycled paper is being employed in a variety of home projects. For example, a mixture of cement and paper, called papercrete, is being used to make bricks for home construction. The blocks are strong and provide excellent insulation from weather and sound. A variety of mixes can be used with lesser or greater amounts of cement, depending on your personal preference and the end result. Using papercrete reduces the need for cement. The bricks made from papercrete can be used to build straight walls, providing a finished product that looks similar to most standard homes. Papercrete can also be used to construct arches and domes. When constructing domes, the need for roofing materials is eliminated, which is another positive attribute to using this building material.

60 Consider Nontraditional Lumber

High-density polyethylene (HDPE), which is made from used milk jugs, juice bottles, and detergent containers, can be recycled into lumber substitutes. This material is generally not used for indoor construction, but it is becoming more and more popular for outdoor decking and fencing. It's a common component of outdoor amenities such as benches, picnic tables, and trashcans. HDPE uses recycled materials, and it doesn't need to be treated to withstand weather and insects like lumber does.

THE CHOICES YOU CAN MAKE . . . **WHEN CHOOSING HOW TO BUILD**

61 Exploit Renewable Resources

Materials that are grown to be harvested are preferable to those whose supply is limited for use in homebuilding and repairs. Examples include wood from forests that are harvested using sustainable methods. These resources are managed so that there is as little impact on the environment as possible. Sustainable products also provide resources and incomes to local populations where they are harvested. The Forest Stewardship Council (FSC) provides third-party certification for wood products. As part of the certification process, the FSC considers all players involved in the harvesting of wood from forest owners to environmental organizations. The organization ensures that the wood is harvested with minimal environmental impact and fair compensation to local businesses and workers.

62 Be a Dumpster Diver—the Art of Salvaging

Interior fixtures can be reused just like external building materials. Salvaging or reusing materials has many advantages. Some people who could not afford antiques inherit vintage material such as beautifully grained wood flooring or heavy steel door handles. When designing a new home or remodeling an existing one, homeowners can contact local salvage companies to see what is available. Many carry an evolving and changing stock of cast-iron bathtubs, oak mantels, and stained-glass windows.

63 Take into Account How Something Was Made

When selecting new materials for building a home, be sure to consider how and where items were made. Does the manufacturer have environmentally sound principles? Do they use recycled materials? Do they recycle their postindustrial materials? Consider using locally produced materials, which eliminates the waste created by transporting the items long distances. This reduces the need to use fossil fuels, and it reduces the impacts of manufacturing and using petroleum products. Whatever the purchase, try to buy items that will last and won't need to be replaced within a few years. Longer-lasting items can be recycled, salvaged, or passed from generation to generation.

64 Get Off the Grid

The national power grid is a network of transmission and distribution systems owned by public companies and investor-owned utilities and cooperatives. Utilities and cooperatives buy and sell power to each other depending on the demand and availability. The network tries to provide redundancy; that means, if there is a problem somewhere in the grid, operations can be rerouted and service can be more easily restored. Harnessing power from nature and reducing energy usage may make it possible to get off the power grid. You can reduce the amount of power you use in your home. From solar to wind and other alternatives, there are a variety of renewable energy options available for keeping lights bright, food cold, and the temperature just right whether your home is on or off the power grid.

65 Get Money for Your Excess Power

If you are generating your own electricity through alternate means, you might be able to work with your local power company to sell any excess energy you produce. You will need to track your electricity usage; your local power provider can tell you what kind of meter you need to install. (We'll talk about two types of meters on page 34.) You can sell your excess energy to the power company through the same network that delivers electricity. How your power company compensates you depends on the type of metering system. Unfortunately,

THE CHOICES YOU CAN MAKE . . . **WHEN CHOOSING HOW TO BUILD** customers are generally paid a lower rate than the retail price for their excess energy. Another alternative is to bank excess power. Rather than selling power to the utility, the homeowner uses it to charge batteries. When the home system is unable to generate electricity, the power stored in the batteries can be accessed.

66 Learn to Meter Your Own Power

Net metering uses the typical meters that are installed on most houses. The meter runs forward when electricity is consumed and backward when electricity is generated. With net metering, excess power is banked for you to access later. This is particularly beneficial for intermittent energy sources such as solar and wind power. The alternative is double metering. One meter measures the electricity used, and the other measures the electricity generated. This method requires the installation of a second meter and can be cumbersome to administer.

67 Get Off the Grid Entirely!

Of course, there's always the potential to get off the grid completely. Most homes that have been able to disconnect from the grid use either solar or wind power. Wind power tends to work better in the winter and worse in the summer, when solar power is at its best, making hybrid systems worth considering.

68 Make Solar Power Work for You

Solar energy is produced when the sun shines on photovoltaic (PV) panels. These panels hold semiconductors that use the sunlight to generate direct current (DC) electricity. Panels are rated in watts, based on the amount of electricity they can produce under ideal sun and temperature conditions. Customers can choose certain panels based on their personal electric demands. Panels are usually mounted on the roof, on steel poles, or on the ground. Local regulations or neighborhood covenants may dictate the location of solar panels. Mounting the panels on the roof requires using the proper supports. It may be necessary to reinforce the roof support to maintain safety and to be in compliance with local building codes. The Web site *www. findsolar.com* is a helpful resource if you are considering installing a home solar system. Beyond explaining monetary savings, the Web site also calculates the amount of greenhouse gas, in carbon dioxide equivalents, that will be saved by going solar.

69 Make Wind Power Work for You

Depending on where you live, wind can provide the means of powering your house. Maps indicating wind energy potential for the country are available to determine if your home is located within an area where wind power would be an effective method of providing power. When choosing an optimal location for a wind turbine, take topography and terrain into account, and consider your local wildlife. Be sure to learn about the local ecology and species habitat and the potential impact your tower might have on your surroundings. The results of your research can minimize negative impacts while providing renewable energy to your home.

70 Harness Wind on Your Property

Even if your home is in an area designated to have appropriate wind speed and resources, you need to consider other factors, such as whether your house is on top of a hill or in a valley. Wind towers can be configured on either horizontal or vertical axes. The horizontal tower is by far the most common, with blades that rotate about an axis that is parallel to the wind. As a result, they must be oriented with the greatest wind direction in mind. Vertical towers are rare and tend to look like eggbeaters. Although their orientation is independent of wind direction, conversion of energy to electricity is less efficient. In either orientation, the blades turn a propeller that captures kinetic energy. A rotor then converts the rotary motion to drive a generator. Unlike a PV used in solar energy, power is captured from moving parts and transferring kinetic energy into electric power.

71 Save Energy When Heating and Cooling

Two of the biggest energy sinks in any home are the heating and cooling systems. The EPA rates heating and cooling systems using the Energy Star logo to promote systems that are more efficient and use less energy. Usually these systems are quieter and have longer lives. Equipment eligible to receive the Energy Star symbol includes boilers, furnaces, heat pumps, programmable thermostats, and air conditioners. Selecting the correct size system for your living space and choosing an efficient model are two crucial ways to save energy. Maintain your current model by cleaning filters, checking ducts for leaks, and installing programmable thermostats to adjust the times the house is heated and cooled throughout the day. Installing a whole-house fan that pulls cool air in and releases warm air through the attic is another effective measure.

72 Choose Efficient Windows and Doors

The bigger a window is, the less efficient it is, and the more windows there are in a house, the more energy it will lose. If you are set on having a window overlooking a scenic vista, you can invest in energy-efficient window models to reduce the negative impact of lost efficiency. Windows that operate using cranks or levers are the most efficient designs, because they allow the window to seal tightly against the frame. Double-hung windows that slide up and down or sideways are less efficient because they must be loose enough to allow sliding, which also means they are loose enough to let air in and out.

73 Go for Double-Pane Windows

Double-pane windows are more efficient than traditional single-pane windows. They are made using two sheets of glass with an air cavity in between. In cold climates, choose windows with the space between the panes filled with argon and the glass covered with a low-emissivity coating so heat reflects back into the living area. In warm climates, choose windows with a similar coating to reflect the heat back outside, preventing it from settling in the house. Unfortunately, the chemicals used to make the coating may be harmful to the environment, causing some of the same problems as pesticides. Additionally, windows with low-emissivity coatings may be more difficult to recycle because the treated glass does not easily fuse with other glasses.

74 Think About the "Seepage"

Air seeping in and out is a major factor with skylights and doors. The standard skylight design has changed, making them more energy efficient. Canister or tube models let light in while eliminating the potential for leaks and heat seepage. Regardless of what type of skylights you get, they need to be installed properly to ensure tight seals. Similarly, check doors to make sure they shut snugly. This keeps the temperature even throughout the rooms inside the house. Doors should fit properly in their frames. You can add magnetic weather stripping to decrease drafts. More important, to reduce the time the compressor or furnace is running, shut the door promptly.

CHAPTER 5

The choices you can make ...

WHEN FURNISHING YOUR HOUSE

75 Keep a Green Home

Once a home is built, you need to furnish it. With the increase in environmental awareness, there are options galore when it comes to filling a home with earth-friendly flooring, furniture, appliances, and lighting. Taking the environment into account won't just help the planet; it can save money through lower electric bills and tax incentives. Making a home green on the inside may just save some green, too.

76 Conserve, Conserve, Conserve

You can conserve natural resources by cutting back on utilities such as power and water. Wasting electricity, for example, wastes money as well as the natural resources that produce the power. The majority of homes use energy produced from coal plants that generate pollutants such as particulate matter, which contributes to health conditions such as asthma, and carbon dioxide, which is a greenhouse gas. So when it comes to furnishing and running a home, if you want to reduce your personal impact, or footprint, on the environment, you can cut back on the energy you burn with the added benefit of saving money.

77 Don't Waste Your Water

Public water supplies usually use groundwater or surface water, like lakes or rivers, as a source. Water is treated and distributed throughout the city. Just like other services provided by a municipality, if more water is demanded, facilities like water treatment plants will either have to be expanded or new facilities will need to be constructed. Water treatment plants are expensive to build and operate. Used water must also be disposed of. The majority of water from residential and commercial toilets, sinks, washing machines, and dishwashers goes to the sanitary sewer and then on to the waste-water treatment plant. There the water is treated before being dis-charged, usually to a bay or stream or other body of water. Although the water is treated, there is concern that it impacts the quality of water into which it is discharged.

78 Make a Goal to Need Fewer Facilities

Not only does conserving power and water save natural resources, it reduces the need to construct costly facilities. As the popula-tion expands, additional power plants, water treatment plants, and wastewater treatment facilities are needed. By conserving resources, the need for additional infrastructure can be postponed or in some cases even eliminated. In many areas of the country, water espe-cially is currently becoming scarce. One way to alleviate strain on the water system is to pipe treated water, called effluent or graywater, to homes and businesses for use in watering lawns and agricultural fields.

79 Put Energy Star Symbols All Around the House

At first, Energy Stars were on just a few pieces, but by 1995 the label-ing was expanded to include other office equipment and residential heating and cooling equipment. In 1996, the Department of Energy jumped onboard and began working with the EPA. The label now appears on more than thirty-five different kinds of products. The Energy Star label means that the appliances were rated objectively, and the label itself includes information on the cost savings for dif-ferent appliances. Many higher-efficiency home appliances may be more expensive than less efficient ones, but consider what the energy savings will be over the life of the appliance when you look at the up-front cost.

THE CHOICES YOU CAN MAKE . . . **WHEN FURNISHING YOUR HOUSE**

80   Make Your Home an Energy Star Home

When energy savings are achieved throughout the house, the entire building can qualify for the Energy Star label. The EPA has published guidelines for a variety of different types of homes, including single-family and multifamily duplexes and apartments; even modular and log homes can qualify. The EPA lists the criteria needed to achieve Energy Star status, such as effective insulation, high-performance windows, tight construction and ducts, efficient heating and cooling equipment, and the use of Energy Star lighting and appliances. In order to complete the certification process, a licensed third party must verify that these standards have been met. The construction of Energy Star homes and the remodeling of older homes to meet Energy Star guidelines has increased as more contractors become familiar with the objectives.

81   Replace Your Bulbs

As grateful as you might be to Thomas Edison for lighting the world, did you know that his incandescent light bulb wastes upward of 95 percent of the energy as heat? This means that the lights are only about 5 percent efficient. That's right—the main reason to flip the switch is light, but really what is being generated is heat. And halogen lights do not fare much better at only 9 percent efficiency. At 20 percent efficiency, compact fluorescent lights (CFLs) are four times more efficient than incandescent lights. If your home is already equipped with incandescent lighting, rather than unscrewing all the bulbs right now and tossing them, simply replace the five lights most frequently used in your home. These lights are most likely in the kitchen, dining room, living room, over the bathroom vanity, and on the front porch.

82 Learn More about CFLs

Compact fluorescent lights (CFLs) are a little more expensive than incandescent bulbs, but they make up for it in longevity and reduced energy use. Over the span of 10,000 hours, a CFL can cost less than half as much energy as an incandescent. In the past CFLs often flickered, but improvements have been made to stop the blinking. New models offer more variety, such as accommodating dimmer switches. Even though most people are in the habit of turning off lights every time they leave a room, that's not a good idea with CFLs. Turning the lights off reduces their life. So unless you are going to be gone for a while, let the light shine. So consider how much you use a room before you install CFLs. You need to choose the right CFL for the job. Talk to your salesperson or check the label on the package to make sure you're making the best selection for your needs.

83 Light Your Home with Better Understanding

Here are a few other energy-saving lighting tips:
- Avoid opaque light shades that require stronger bulbs.
- Use light paints and flooring to reflect light.
- Clean dust from light fixtures so their light will shine through.
- When reading or performing tasks requiring focused lighting, turn off background lights and rely on a small focused lamp.

84 Now Consider These Appliances

Most kitchen appliances use water and electricity or natural gas, so buying energy-efficient models conserves two of the three. When considering kitchen appliances, look for the Energy Star symbol. While the initial cost of the appliance may be higher than ones without the star symbol, the energy savings throughout the life of the appliance will more than cover the additional purchase expense. If you take into account the initial purchase price, maintenance costs, and operational costs for a large appliance, you can expect to save about $200 a year; over an expected operating life of five to ten years this results in considerable savings. One other way to reduce energy consumption is to stop using unnecessary appliances, such as an extra stand-alone freezer that runs year-round. This is an easy step that can save a lot of money!

85 Investigate the Impact of Wooden Floors

Older flooring options had little to do with environmental impact and more with aesthetics, but that approach has changed. When picking flooring, people often consider both their health and the environment. Wooden flooring first came on the scene during the baroque period, around the late 1600s. But by the late 1800s and early 1900s, mass production and Victorian standards made wood the norm for flooring. Over the years, its popularity has waxed and waned. Today, wood is again a popular flooring alternative.

86 Think about Where That Wood Comes from

Wooden flooring generally comes from domestic, exotic, or non-domestic forests. Wooden flooring can also be re-milled from other wood products and older flooring. Although hardwood flooring is a renewable resource, you need to be aware of the source of the wood you are considering. Domestic flooring does not require the extensive shipping of exotics. Exotic wood is sometimes harvested from forests where conditions of the local ecology and population are not taken into account. This is especially true when low prices and competition encourage irresponsible harvesting. Look for the Forest

Stewardship Council (FSC) stamp of approval on wood and let it be a determining factor in your selection. The FSC is an international organization that works to promote responsible stewardship of the earth's forests by bringing together timber users, local foresters, and human rights and environmental organizations.

87 Look into Laminate Floors

Laminate, which mimics the traditional wooden floor, has become a popular option. It provides the same benefits as wooden floors, with a reduction in sealants and the potential for better harvesting practices. Many more styles are available today. Laminate floors are easier to install than wooden floors, and many projects can be done by homeowners over a long weekend. Floating-type flooring offers planks with tongue-and-groove construction, making the planks easier to lock in place over the existing sub-floor. Some designs, however, do require the use of glue. Laminate floors are also durable and easy to maintain.

88 Consider Tile and Stone

Like wood, tile and stone offer low-allergen amenities. Their smooth surfaces are not conducive to a thriving dust mite population and can be cleaned easily, unlike carpet. Another consideration is durability. Stone and tile can last for decades, meaning that manufacturing resources are conserved. Depending on the sources of the tile and stone, there can be environmental impacts, however. The EPA requires mines to implement best management practices to avoid affecting storm water and surface water in the area. Mine reclamation, or repairing the damage to mined lands, is more common now. In addition, depending on how far tile and stone are shipped, they can weigh heavily in terms of the impacts from transportation.

89   Ponder the Entire Process—Tile and Stone

Tile is often made from clay mined throughout the United States. The demand for decorative floor tiles has grown, resulting in more sophisticated automation processes within the industry. Many tile manufacturers use recycled tiles, glass, and even carpet or plastic fibers in their stock. Clear, brown, and green glass can be recycled and used to produce solid-color and decoratively designed tiles. Stone flooring comes in a variety of shapes and sizes, from pebbles to large slabs. Stone flooring offers consumers a choice of numerous patterns and colors. Stone used in flooring is usually made of porcelain, limestone, marble, or granite. It is installed using relatively benign mortar and grout. As with wood, laminates are now made that mimic stone and tile flooring. Also like wood laminate, these floorings are produced with tongue-and-groove edges and can be installed to float above the existing floor.

90   Consider the Carpet Conundrum

While carpet provides more padding and is softer to walk and sit on than wood or tile, it also harbors dirt, dust mites, and other allergens such as mold. To avoid allergic reactions to dust mites, carpets must be vacuumed regularly. There is also concern that carpets emit volatile organics and collect pesticides tracked in from outside and indoor contaminants. As other products have included recycled material in their feedstock, so has carpet. Some manufacturers rely solely on recycled plastics to produce flooring. Several different brands are made from recycled soda bottles, for example. Because this production relies on post-consumer material, it avoids disposal of waste products in landfills and incinerators. When choosing flooring options, you may be surprised how many recycled products are available.

THE CHOICES YOU CAN MAKE . . . **WHEN FURNISHING YOUR HOUSE**

91 Try an Alternate Flooring Material

Relatively new to the flooring world are sustainable cork and bamboo. Cork flooring can be installed in much the same way as laminate and can be manufactured in a variety of colors and appearances, including a natural cork appearance. It can even be made to look like stone or tile. Because cork is giving and flexible, it can be installed on floors that aren't completely level, making it particularly useful in older homes where portions of the floor may have already settled. When choosing cork flooring, check to see that it's formaldehyde-free and that any varnish is water-based. Bamboo is actually a grass that grows like a weed. The majority of bamboo is grown in China and India, so the environmental impacts from shipping can offset the benefits of using this type of flooring. When manufactured for durable flooring, bamboo maintains the appearance of hardwood, but it can be tinted different colors. Because it is wood, bamboo requires sealants and protective waxes. Shoppers and installers can check to see that sealants and waxes with little or no volatile organic compounds are used. Companies such as EcoTimber (*www.ecotimber.com*) manufacture bamboo that is made using European adhesive, which is lower in volatile organics.

92 Conserve Energy in the Bathroom

Along with improvements to other appliances, great strides have been made in manufacturing more water-conserving toilets. It is estimated that about one-quarter of the water used in an average home goes to flushing the toilet if efficient toilets aren't installed. Homes built before 1992 that haven't had any improvements made are likely to have an old-fashioned 3.6 gallons per flush (gpf) model toilets. Newer models use only 1.5 gallons per flush, and the future may hold even more efficient flushers. This reduces the amount of

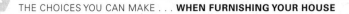

water being pumped from aquifers and streams, treated, and piped to the house, and also saves on treating and discharging the used water, too.

93 Change the Way You Shower

Beyond taking shorter and colder showers, you can take other steps to conserve water and natural resources while cleaning up. Standard showerheads put out up to 5 gallons per minute (gpm). Low-flow showerheads can cut that in half. If a low-flow shower isn't satisfactory, try using an aerator showerhead. Air is added to the water as it flows from the head, making it feel like a higher flowing showerhead. You can also add aerators to spigots, reducing a flow of more than 2 gpm to about 1 gpm. Aerators are relatively inexpensive and easy to install.

94 Make Forward Thinking Furniture Choices

Run-of-the-mill stuffed furniture, much like mattresses, contains fire-retardant chemicals and formaldehyde. Although regulators have said that the protection afforded by the retardants ranks higher than the potential risk of chemical health problems, you may opt to purchase less chemically protected furniture. Organically grown ramie and cotton are available for upholstering furniture. These materials are beautiful to look at and comfortable to sit on, and those with chemical sensitivities may find it a salvation to home furnishing. Wood furniture should have the FSC seal to ensure it was forested with the environment and indigenous cultures in mind. Other companies collect old wood, salvaging it from demolition sites, and reworking it to make new wood furniture of both contemporary and more nostalgic styles. One example is Cabin Furniture and Décor (*www.1cabinfurniture.com*), where you can buy hutches, benches, and dining-room tables and chairs made from reclaimed lumber.

CHAPTER 6

The choices you can make . . .

WHEN IN YOUR COMMUNITY

95 Get Involved!

Sometimes in groups, sometimes as individuals, people have worked to promote change. They have bucked the status quo in an effort to make things better either for themselves or for others. The list of people who have made a difference is lengthy, but one individual is worth highlighting. John Muir, considered the original preservationist and father of the national park system, spread the conviction that people need natural space to thrive. Muir helped found the Sierra Club and lobbied politicians against the destruction of resources in the Pacific Northwest. His legacy lives on in numerous schools and protected wilderness areas that bear his name.

96 Learn to Be an Activist

The list of people who have inspired change continues to grow, and one interesting point about nearly all of them is that they weren't born into activism. Something happened in their lives that drove them to work for change. People can be at the forefront of a movement or they can be in the ranks providing support; either way, individuals and groups can make a difference and redirect the course of history. Dr. Rosalie Bertel is a good example. As a mathematician and nun in the order of the Grey Nuns of the Sacred Heart, Dr. Bertel was spurred to action in the mid-1980s after the nuclear reactor meltdown in Chernobyl and the Union Carbide explosion in Bhopal, India. She has become a respected scholar and author and now works on behalf of Native Americans and Gulf War veterans on the effects of depleted uranium and low-level radiation. Like Dr. Bertel, lead by example and you will teach and touch many people.

97 Get in Touch with the People in Charge

One of the most important political moves you can make is to vote. Politicians are elected as representatives, and they generally work to promote the beliefs of their constituents—the people they represent and the people who elected them. Before going to the polling precinct, make sure you have done your homework. To get the most from your vote, know the issues and where the candidates stand. If you want to bring attention to a local issue or if you need a question answered, you can contact your local political leaders and regulators. Contact information should be in the phone book or available on the municipality's or agency's Web site.

98 Identify the Lawmakers

At times, a particular issue is decided by individual states, not by the federal government. In that case, state lawmakers have more influence. If you aren't sure who your representatives or senators are, look up your state government's Web site. It will have information regarding your lawmakers and how to contact them. The senators and representatives are elected by district. They may have a local office in their district or an office in the state's capital. Depending on the schedule and availability of the legislature, you may receive a call back from an aide rather than the lawmaker you originally contacted. The Web site *www.speakout.com* has a wealth of information on all aspects of the legislative process and the best ways to communicate with legislators. The site also contains additional information on political activism.

99 Face a Federal Matter

If the issue is on a federal level, you can contact your U. S. senator or representative. Each state has two senators. States are divided by population into districts, and each district has a representative. However, rather than dealing directly with your senator or representative, you will most likely be in contact with one of their assistants. Work to build a rapport with this person because he or she will likely have a good understanding of the issues and will probably have more time to look into an issue.

100 Take Time with Your Correspondence

It's good to remember that written or e-mailed communication is likely to be considered public record, and this includes e-mail addresses. You'll get further with legislators if you have a well-crafted letter or e-mail. Here is a list of tips for contacting a member of the legislature:

- Check your spelling, grammar, and punctuation when writing an e-mail or a letter.
- Limit your written correspondence to one page and address only one topic per letter or e-mail.
- Back up any claims or assertions with facts. If necessary, attach references.
- If you would like to visit your legislator, make an appointment first. Again, offer a single-page fact sheet on the issue and stick to the topic.

101 Hold a Public Hearing

Rather than acting on behalf of a legislative issue that is already being processed, you can also request a public hearing on a local issue. For example, you might request a hearing to inform the public of the potential impacts a new development could have on nearby wetlands. Your letter would include a summary of the project and details about how it will impact the area. In this example, you would describe the development project and specifically how it would impact the wetlands. Through the Freedom of Information Act, you can obtain specific information on the project from the regulatory agency responsible for its permitting. Keep in mind that if you are requesting a public hearing, you should be prepared to make a presentation. Your facts should be in order and organized. Practice your presentation well ahead of time; it may just be the beginning of a political career.

102 Contact Your Local Regulator

You can write to regulators who are responsible for permitting and monitoring activities. This could range from a letter to the Federal Drug Administration (FDA) regarding animal testing or to the EPA regarding a nearby superfund site. As with other letters, the tone should be respectful, and while the issue may be emotional, try to present facts. For example, if you are writing a letter to the FDA, you could request that animal testing no longer be used to determine cosmetic ingredient safety and that other means be used. While the plight of animals used in laboratory testing can be emotional, be sure to emphasize the accuracy and availability of alternative measures. You should also include any applicable laws and regulations pertaining to the issue. Even though many of the issues concerning the environment are emotional, it's important to understand the laws and regulations.

103 Alert the Media

If there's an issue that needs to be covered, contact local media outlets. Media coverage is a good way to reach a wider audience, but the media can't cover an event or an issue unless they know about it. Many newspapers, radio stations, and television stations list their directories online, making it easier to find contact information. If you get in touch with a specific reporter, determine if the person is aware of the issue and if he or she needs any additional information. If you don't believe the media has covered a story fairly, contact the editor or a manager. Be sure to list the specific items you took issue with and provide correct facts. Remember that an ongoing relationship with the media is desirable and that bullying them won't help that relationship.

104 Write an Article Yourself

If you want to see your name in print, write a letter to the editor of the newspaper. Make sure to follow the format required by the newspaper, especially with respect to length and personal information. The letter should be timely and concise, and even though it will go through an editor, make sure to proof it for spelling and grammar. If the letter covers a heated issue, consider how you will feel when it's published in the paper with your name attached. The newspaper may not publish the first letter it gets on a topic, but if a topic appears again and again—especially if it's a concern voiced by several writers—it's likely to be recognized. If you have more to say than can be communicated in a 200-word letter, you can compose a longer piece, such as an op-ed article.

105 Write to a Specific Company

Letters to companies could range from encouraging them to take a specific action to requesting that they stop a certain practice. There are generally two approaches to letting a company know you are concerned with its activities and would like to see some changes. You can write a letter as an individual or you can send a letter from a collaborative group, addressed directly to board members. The letter should describe the specific issues of concern and request certain actions as a result. Also, request that the company respond to the letter and explain its stance on the issue. Send the letter by certified mail so you receive a receipt that it was delivered, preferably knowing who signed for it. If the first letter doesn't get a response, consider writing again.

106 Use the Power of Shareholders

Another method of communicating with companies is through their shareholders. Shareholders own part of a company and have certain rights and privileges. They can request a meeting with the board of directors or attend a shareholders' meeting. They vote on company issues either in person or through mailed ballots. Combining the efforts of other shareholders can also prove effective in changing corporate policies and actions. An alternative approach is if a public pension fund invests in a company you take issue with, work with the pension fund and its members to sway company policies. Another alternative is to determine if a university has a vested interest in a company. Perhaps you can persuade those in charge to reconsider their investments. The larger the stockholder, the louder the message.

107 Join a Movement—Whether It's Big or Small

If you want to protect the environment with others, you can join a cause, an organization, a church, or even a political party. It may be that there is already a group working on behalf of a cause that interests you. This could be either a local group dealing with a very specific issue or an international group that takes on many issues at a time. By joining, you will meet other like-minded people, and you will learn a great deal about the politics and activities in the area. This offers the chance to network and may even lead to other activities and endeavors.

108 Support Politics with a Green Party

Protecting the environment can be a very political issue. The foundation of the Green Party of the United States is based primarily on environmentalism and social justice. Similarly, the Greens/Green Party USA also promotes sustainability and a balance between people and nature. While these two parties focus primarily on the environment and other social issues, these issues are increasingly becoming a part of the platforms of more mainstream political parties. You can consider joining a political organization in your area or volunteering for a candidate who makes the environment an important aspect of his or her campaign. You may be able to meet like-minded people in your area online at Web sites of political and activist organizations.

109 Spearhead a Cause

If you have looked around and there just isn't an organization that seems to fit with your beliefs, or if a specific issue has come up that hasn't been addressed publicly before, you can consider spearheading a cause of your own. The Michigan Land Use Institute offers activists a tool kit for getting people involved. The group offers a variety of sample documents, including a sample Freedom of Information Act letter, a sample news release, and samples of testimony letters on their Web site at *www.mlui.org.*

110 Use the Internet to Your Advantage

Web sites are a great way to disseminate information to the masses and link up with other organizations. Creating a Web site is not something everyone feels comfortable with, so it might be worthwhile to search out other group members willing to do it for free. Some Web site designers work regularly with nonprofits, usually charging lower rates than for-profit companies. Web sites should provide up-to-date information on the organization and contact information. The Internet is also a way to set up regular communications with members through e-mail lists, bulletin boards, and blogs. Online petitions can be developed that tally responses and send them on to recipients, such as politicians and corporate leaders. A Web site can be used not just to advertise an organization, but also to allow back-and-forth communication between members and others looking for information. NetAction assists activists with communicating via the Internet. Its Web site (*www.netaction.org*) includes tips on making good use of the Internet and using e-mail as a primary method of communication.

111 Demonstrate What You Want

Well-run demonstrations can be vital tools in getting the word out to people, sending a message to politicians and community leaders, and giving credibility to a cause. Here are some tips for getting the most out of a demonstration:

- Contact the local media well in advance and then follow up with reminder e-mails or phone calls.
- Post flyers strategically in areas where they will be well received.
- Consider contacting another organization to attend. Be prepared to reciprocate when the request is made.
- Prepare signs to convey the message. Make sure there are enough!
- Have a catchy chant ready to call attention to the demonstration.
- Be prepared to speak. And if possible, try to schedule community leaders or other activists to speak as well.
- If the demonstration involves a march or a walk, clear it through the proper channels. The finish line should be festive and, if possible, it should have booths from other organizations to offer support and show solidarity.
- Invite vendors to sell T-shirts and bumper stickers. They should pay an entry fee and/or a percentage of their sales.

112 Use Television as a Tool

Many cable networks provide local access channels at no cost. You will need to contact the cable provider to find out what is available and what the requirements are for getting on the air. Airtime can be used to show a video made by a larger organization or produced by the local organization. The station will likely have requirements for the video's content and format. The network will most likely provide minimal advertising for the program, so publicize the show as you would a demonstration. Other ways of getting the word out include newspaper advertisements and announcements in special interest newsletters. Or you could bring together others to watch a special video or movie at someone's house or in a larger facility. Professionally produced movies could be used to spearhead a more local issue. By watching the movie together, members can discuss the relevant issues, how they apply locally, and the actions to be taken. Having a theme and asking attendees to bring along a potluck dish to share can add a little creativity.

CHAPTER 7

The choices you can make . . .

WHEN AT WORK

113 Run Your Office More Efficiently

If you operate a business, you can run it more efficiently and green things up a bit. Any changes you intend to implement will more than likely require a formal plan or program or, at a minimum, a memo (preferably an electronic one to keep the use of paper to a minimum). Although some programs may have a cost associated with getting them up and running, once started they will most likely save energy or the environment and wind up reducing operating costs as well. In addition, businesses can promote their green actions to potential customers and future employees.

114 Make Your Product More Green

If you manufacture a product, consider revising operations to meet the criteria for fair or organic trade. For example, Pacific Natural Foods—an Oregon-based company whose product line includes soups, broths, beverages, and ready-made meals—shows its commitment to environmental responsibility in its procurement and packaging efforts. Although Pacific Natural Foods are sold throughout the United States, the company tries to get its ingredients from local farms to reduce the amount of fossil fuels required to ship the food. The company also works diligently with manufacturers to reduce waste and design the most efficient and environmentally friendly packaging.

115 Get Certified!

The federal government began constructing Leadership in Energy and Environmental Design (LEED) certified buildings in the 1990s; the private sector soon followed. Proper and efficient lighting is one of the LEED design goals, and it makes good business sense, too. Certification lets others know that business owners care about the environment, and it sets an example for other businesses. Apply for any awards that might be available locally or statewide. Consider joining or starting a recycling or green organization in the community where people can share information they have learned while improving their office operations. Submit articles on your efforts to local newspaper and magazines. To raise the bar in your area of business, go green and watch others follow.

116 Get Employees to Buy In

If you expect to successfully make changes at work, it's best to get your employees to buy in to the concept. Employees will probably be administering the programs, and they may have some inventive ideas. Employees who came from university environments or former employers where sustainable living was promoted may have worked with campus or workplace programs. They may also have experience in their personal lives, at their homes, or in their communities. Employees who feel they've been included in a plan or program are more likely to cooperate.

117 Figure Out What It Means for Your Employees

Employees are more likely to accept changes and new policies where they really see and feel they have ownership in the company, not because they've been told their values matter. This often means breaking down barriers between departments and levels and bringing everyone into the fold. Sometimes all it takes is acknowledging the cost and environmental impact for employees to look at operations just a little differently. Think about rewarding employees who offer suggestions on ways to save or implement programs in their own departments. Make good examples of employees advocating greener operations.

118 Take a Look at What Your Office Is Wasting

Here are some common ways to reduce waste in the office:

- Reduce paper. Encourage employees to use electronic means to work and communicate. Make double-sided copies for handouts at meetings to conserve the amount of paper you use.
- You will inevitably have to use some paper, so start a recycling program.
- Choose your printer inks and toners carefully. Reuse and refill toners; recycle ink cartridges.
- Reuse office equipment. If you choose to upgrade your computer system, you'll be left with fully functioning machines that still have a lot of life in them. Donate them to charities or give them back to your supplier instead of throwing them away.
- Cut down on disposable products. If your business has a kitchen, cafeteria, or coffee machine, encourage employees to bring their own mugs and silverware.
- Reuse boxes and other shipping and packaging materials.
- Reuse old envelopes for interoffice mail.

119 Look into an Energy Audit

A first step in the direction of reducing the company's impact on the environment is to have an energy audit done for the facility. The local power company may offer to perform an audit for a modest fee or possibly for free, or you may have to contract with an energy expert. You may spend some in the beginning, but you'll save money in the end. When hiring a contractor to perform an energy audit, make sure you know what you are signing up for. A preliminary audit includes just a walk-through with recommendations. A general audit goes further and includes a review of expenses. An investment audit will calculate the return on investment that can be expected, allowing businesses to budget building and operation renovations. A professional energy auditor will have more recommendations than one from a utility and will mostly include construction or material suggestions. After the audit, you will have to decide which and when improvements can be made or schedule them into the capital-improvement budget.

120 Do Your Own Energy Assessment

Before bringing in an energy expert, you can do your own energy walk-through, taking note of the following things:

- Is natural lighting utilized as much as possible?
- Can incandescent lights be replaced with compact fluorescent lamps or halogen lamps?
- Can green power be purchased from the local utility?
- Is the office equipment (i.e., computers, printers, fax machines) Energy Star rated?
- Are computers set to go to sleep?
- Are employees encouraged to turn off their computers, printers, and lights at the end of the day or if they will be gone for a few hours?
- Are outdoor windows and doors kept closed?
- If windows are not low-e, have they been treated for energy efficiency?
- Is a comfortable temperature maintained for most employees?
- Is it understood that some employees may occasionally need to don a sweater to warm up or use a fan to cool off?

121 Reduce Paper and Ink—It's Possible!

Since the onset of personal computers, the amount of paper generated has skyrocketed. Not only is paper a waste product, it's expensive to buy and diminishes natural resources. By reducing the amount of paper used in the office, you can reduce the amount of paper needed to be stored and delivered. Come up with milestone goals for the percentage reduction in paper used. Encourage employees to think first before printing and make sure all documents are spell-checked and formatted correctly so they don't have to be printed again. When making copies, double-side the documents. If you are producing handouts for a meeting, consider whether they are really necessary. When audiovisuals are used, paper handouts are usually superfluous. If handouts are a must, consider printing double pages on a single side of paper.

122 Encourage Employees to Enlist in Change

Determine which activities can be accomplished by your employees through online programs rather than generating a paper trail. Office supplies can be ordered, conference or training requests submitted, and even timesheets and expense reports can be completed online. This saves time, eliminating the need to shuttle paper from one desk to another, and it saves resources, too. Other ways to cut back while maintaining a professional appearance include minimizing margins, decreasing font size, and eliminating double-spacing. These minor changes will add up over time, especially when printing large documents.

123 Think More about Ink

Printers may be inexpensive, but cartridges are not. Ink can be a costly part of any office operation. There are a number of ways to reduce its use. When printing a document that is not final, print it in draft mode. The draft mode on your printer uses approximately 50 percent of the ink used in normal print mode. You can buy software that allows more control over the amount of ink a printer uses. Although using the software may not save as much ink as printing in draft mode, it does offer some in-between options.

124 Change the Way the Company Travels

Even with the advent of online meetings and teleconferencing, people are still flying and driving an extensive amount. If a trip out of the office is necessary, consider more fuel-efficient ways of traveling or combining trips to nearby locales or with other meetings. Sometimes, juggling a schedule can reduce travel from two trips to one. When it comes to getting employees to and from work, encourage the use of mass transit and carpools. Employers can provide tax-advantage spending accounts for employees to cover the cost of riding the bus, train, or subway. These programs allow employees to pay for mass transit with pre-tax dollars using a convenient pass or card that's ordered online. Also, employers can provide special parking spots for people who carpool.

125 Promote Smart Cars and Telecommuting

Choose energy-efficient vehicle or hybrids as your company cars or fleet vehicles. Companies will feel the savings on multiple cars more than individuals. This will save money, and it sets an example of conservation and environmental protection at a corporate level. Telecommuting has also become popular and saves on more than transportation costs. Some companies are set up for telecommuting, using field representatives or contractors who work out of their houses. Besides avoiding going in to the office, there are other benefits of working from home. Depending on the company dress code, allowing employees to work from home can decrease the cost and environmental impact from dry cleaning.

126 Make All Those Office Supplies Green

When it comes to making purchases for the company, buy green. Almost any office supply is available in recycled or organic versions, from sticky notes to calendars. Large office-supply retailers carry a variety of recycled-content paper products including folders and pencils. Other more specialized stores such as Green Earth Office Supply raise the bar for environmentally friendly supplies and equipment. They carry everything from hole punches made from recycled steel to hemp planners.

127 Green the Day-to-Day Operations

Consider all the different processes that make up the day-to-day operations of the company and you will realize that little steps add up. When sending out mailings that need to be returned, use reusable envelopes. If possible, reuse envelopes you receive. If giving out promotional gifts, make sure they are made out of recycled material. Review everyday practices for mailings and cut out any waste in the process. Can packages going to different people at the same address be combined? Can packages from different departments be shipped together? It may take some additional communication, but with support that travels all the way up the corporate ladder, savings can be seen in this area.

128 Appoint a Recycling Coordinator

There are so many options and venues for recycling at the office that it's a good idea to appoint one person as the recycling coordinator. This could be the same person who conducted the waste assessment or audit, but depending on the size of the business, this doesn't necessarily need to be his or her only responsibility. This coordinator should be someone who is enthusiastic about recycling and either is already familiar with the company's waste management practices or is willing to jump right in—so to speak. Explain that he or she will be responsible for preparing a plan, educating coworkers, and determining a method for evaluating performance.

129 Collaborate with the Offices Around You

If your office does not generate a lot of one particular kind of recyclable, it might work best to combine efforts with other offices in the area. Also look into participating in a cooperative that could get better prices in purchasing recycling equipment and could be the difference between paying to have your recyclables picked up and making money from them. Smaller haulers may also be available at better rates than larger haulers for taking away materials. If your business is located in a rural area, you may not be able to join a co-op or a use mom-and-pop hauler. In this case, secondhand hauling could be used. When office supplies or another item is delivered to the office, the hauler may be able to take the recyclables to a recycling facility for you. This works best if the truck is usually empty on return trips, allowing the driver room to haul and the potential to make a little extra money.

130 Recycle Office Items

Some common office items that can be recycled include:

- Aluminum cans
- Batteries (Better yet, use rechargeable batteries.)
- Cardboard boxes
- Computers
- Glass
- Ink cartridges
- Magazines
- Paper
- Plastics

As the recycling program continues, solicit ideas and suggestions from your employees as to how they think it's working out. Share the problems and successes experienced with the program with them as well. Let employees know if contaminants are making their way into the waste stream and what the impacts from those contaminants are. The quantities of recycling being performed should be shared along with any revenue generated. Consider donating the revenue to an employee program, such as a scholarship, or to a local charity.

CHAPTER 8

The choices you can make . . .

WHEN GETTING FROM HERE TO THERE

131 Believe the Hype about Hybrids

A hybrid is a combination of two separate things—in the case of automobiles, an engine and a motor. A hybrid car uses both an electric motor and a gasoline engine. Both the engine and motor have favorable and less savory qualities, but when working together they bring out the best in each other. Cars that are strictly electric have to be recharged at regular intervals, and without the horses under the hood, they're not good at high speeds. But electric cars do well at low speeds and produce fewer to no emissions. Gasoline-powered cars have the pickup most drivers are accustomed to, and they can be conveniently fueled. However, gasoline isn't the cleanest fuel. Producing it isn't good for the environment and neither is burning it.

132 Understand How Hybrids Work

In hybrid vehicles, the electric and gasoline systems work together, using each other's best aspects. The gas engine can charge the batteries. Hybrids capture the energy produced during braking, so they don't have to be plugged in to recharge their batteries. Because gasoline motors are so inefficient at low speeds, the electric motors kick in during stop-and-go traffic, significantly reducing the amount of fuel burned and emissions produced. For skeptics who are concerned that hybrid-car batteries are too expensive to replace and dispose of, rest assured. Ford, Honda, and Toyota claim that the batteries in their hybrids will last the life of the vehicle. When it comes to disposal, the batteries can be recycled just like any other car battery.

133 Look at the Difference

Hybrids, when compared to their gasoline-powered counterparts, get about 20 to 35 percent better gas mileage, but the improved fuel efficiency may not make up for the increased sticker price. To get a good idea before you sign your check, take a look at the Web site *www.fueleconomy.gov*, run by the Department of Energy and the Environmental Protection Agency (EPA). It allows browsers to do their own comparisons and view emissions statistics. The price of a hybrid might be higher, but it also includes the cost of developing new technology.

134 Consider the Emissions

The fuel efficiency and price of the car aren't the only things to consider when buying a greener car. Hybrids produce much fewer emissions than cars that run strictly on gasoline. According to the fuel economy Web site, the Honda Civic will produce about 5.5 tons per year of greenhouse gases, or carbon dioxide equivalents, while the Honda Civic Hybrid will produce 3.7 tons per year.

135 Face the Biodiesel Facts

Diesel fuel is produced as part of the process of refining regular gasoline. Diesel fuel gets better gas mileage than standard gasoline and produces less carbon dioxide. Unfortunately, diesel releases a lot of particulate matter that gets stuck in people's noses and lungs, even impacting the body's ability to transfer oxygen to the blood. That's where biodiesel comes in. Made from renewable resources such as vegetable oil, animal fats, even used cooking oil, biodiesel uses alcohol to separate nonfuel components from fat. Production ranges from full-scale facilities to home kits that can be built and operated in the backyard. By-products of the process include glycerol—the same ingredient that's used in making soap, toothpaste, food, and cosmetics—and seed meal that can be used in livestock feed.

136 Power Up—Electric Cars

There's an ongoing debate about whether the electric car is really dead. After being promoted in the late 1990s, cars running strictly on electricity have been steered off the road. However, they found

THE CHOICES YOU CAN MAKE . . . **WHEN GETTING FROM HERE TO THERE**

new uses on golf courses and at tourist destinations. Many cities and even amusement parks use electric buses or shuttles for moving people around. Because buses work on set times and routes, the time needed to charge them is incorporated into their routine schedules.

137 Try a Flexible-Fuel Vehicle

Flexible-fuel vehicles, or FFVs, are made to run on a mixture of gasoline and an alternate fuel such as ethanol or methanol. Standard gasoline engines can't operate using flex fuels, but FFVs can burn both—and that's what makes them so flexible. There are a variety of FFVs on the market, including sedans, trucks, and sport utility vehicles. Ethanol—otherwise known as ethyl alcohol, grain alcohol, or moonshine—leads the way in replacing a portion of the gasoline. It's made by distilling a fermented brew of corn, yeast, sugar, and water. Other plants, such as switchgrass, are being considered as corn substitutes. It takes one bushel of corn to produce two and a half gallons of ethanol. There is concern that the environmental impact from growing plants to produce ethanol (i.e., from the use of fertilizers, pesticides, and transporting plants to processing facilities) outweighs the benefits of burning cleaner fuels.

138 Consider an Alternative-Fuel Vehicle

Where FFVs rely on ethanol and methanol as a fuel component, alternative-fuel vehicles (AFVs) rely on a combination of gasoline and either compressed natural gas (CNG) or liquefied petroleum gas (LPG). As with other alternatives, fueling station locations are spotty across the United States. Most AFVs on the road were converted from standard gasoline-powered engines. Tax incentives encourage companies to convert their fleets and private individuals to convert their personal cars. Some states even allow drivers of certified AFVs to use high-occupancy lanes.

THE CHOICES YOU CAN MAKE . . . **WHEN GETTING FROM HERE TO THERE**

139 Be Your Own Motor

With environmental and health concerns as primary factors, more people are biking and walking. Drivers take 1.1 billion trips every day. Based on information collected by the Bureau of Transportation Statistics, the majority of those trips, about 87 percent, are taken in personal vehicles. If each driver cut out one trip a day—or even a few a week—it would save up to 25 percent of the fossil fuels used for personal transportation. Walking usually takes more time than driving. Still, if you are looking to do the planet (and your body) a favor, you can walk to grocery store for milk or to a friend's house for a visit.

140 Learn to Enjoy Walking

When opting to walk instead of drive, there are a few things you can do to make it more comfortable. Quick-drying clothing means no more sweaty shirts, and carrying a water bottle will keep you hydrated. Lightweight daypacks are great for toting items that will be taken along or picked up on errands. Consider safety when you choose to walk. Choose a route that's well lighted and pedestrian friendly, and take a cell phone. Even though you aren't driving, it's a good idea to take a driver's license or other form of identification.

141 Bike—It's Good for You and the Planet

Biking is good exercise, and one trip on the bike saves one trip in a car. Many cities are not set up for safe biking, but improvements are being made. For example, the city of Davis, California, boasts more bicycles than cars with its wide streets and network of bike paths. Davis's mild climate and gentle terrain encourages bike travel, which the city estimates makes up 20 to 25 percent of all trips. Legislation like the Bicycle Commuter Act, introduced in 2005, encourages employers to support bicycle commuting by offering tax incentives. The costs of bike commuting, such as lights and bike repair and maintenance, are also covered. If you choose to bike, know the laws in their area and be careful when sharing the road with cars.

142 Use Mass Transit

Mass transit helps reduce the number of cars on the road. Numbers vary, but the Maryland Department of Transportation estimates that a full bus eliminates sixty cars from the road and that translates to reduced emissions to the air and runoff to streams and creeks. You can find out more about the bus service in your area by contacting the local transit authority or by looking online for schedules and routes. Taking the bus allows riders time to read, listen to music, and even catch up on sleep on the way to work or school. Bus rides can also be substitutes for long car trips. Greyhound and Trailways buses travel across the country, allowing riders to check out vistas along the way. Before making a trip, ask about meal stops and consider bringing along a pillow and snacks to make the trip more enjoyable.

143 If You Have to Drive, Don't Go It Alone

If you live in an area where riding mass transit isn't feasible but still want to take a car or two off the road, consider carpooling. A number of Web sites match destinations and drivers looking to save money and vehicle use. Check out sites like *www.erideshare.com*, *www.carpoolconnect.com*, *www.icarpool.com*, and *www.rideshareonline.com*. Ridesharing offers companionship and a break from always having to be behind the wheel, plus many states have carpool lanes. These lanes allow high-occupancy vehicles to sidestep traffic for a less congested ride.

144 Follow the Rules of the Carpool

Depending on how long the commute is, riders may be spending a lot of time together, so it's best to set a few rules at the get-go:

- Will drivers and riders meet at someone's house or a common location such as a parking lot?
- Will anyone be smoking?
- Is eating in the car okay?
- Are stops acceptable?
- Will there be a set wait time if someone is late?

145 Share a Car

Car sharing has increased as well, and there are a variety of programs available. Businesses such as Zipcar (*www.zipcar.com*) and Flexcar (*www.flexcar.com*) operate in numerous cities across the United States, including New York, Chicago, and Los Angeles. Cooperatives like City Carshare (*www.citycarshare.org*) in San Francisco operate as nonprofits. With car-sharing programs, members pay a monthly fee or hourly rates and have access to a variety of cars and trucks. You choose whatever vehicle suits your fancy, a truck for that trip to the lumberyard or a sedan for a night out with friends. Most programs offer a fleet of hybrid and low-emission vehicles, too.

146 Scoot to Your Destination

Scooter sales are skyrocketing as people look for a break from high gas prices. Prices for gas-powered scooters range from $1,000 to $10,000; fuel ratings for gas-powered scooters run 50 miles to the gallon or better. There's a true distinction in size and power; smaller scooters are slower and not as powerful. New larger scooters compare to motorcycles in price and power while still offering a low mileage alternative. Unlike motorcycles, scooters allow drivers to sit upright. Electric scooters range from the fold-up push scooter to full sit-down models. Unlike gas-powered scooters, electrics are allowed on mass transit, making a commute to the bus stop a little quicker. At a sticker price of $500 or less, they're much cheaper. Depending on what riders need, electric scooters can be an excellent way to get across campus or to the train depot. When it comes to the environment, no exhaust means no air pollution. With proper maintenance and operation, battery life spans increase.

147 Improve Mileage and Reduce Emissions

Consider this: The National Highway Traffic and Safety Administration calculated that the average vehicle mileage increased only 1.6 miles per gallon (mpg), from 23.1 mpg in 1980 to 24.7 mpg in 2004. The improvement could have been larger, but the huge successes of SUVs, relatively inexpensive gas, and more people idling in traffic brought down the mileage calculations (but did not decrease emissions). When you drive, you can take steps to increase mileage and even reduce emissions.

148 Improve Efficiency

Until zero-impact cars or fuels are invented, here's a list of things you can do to improve fuel efficiency:

- Aggressive driving, including rapid acceleration off the line, wastes gas and increases emissions. Maintaining a smooth—and legal—pace will get you more miles to the gallon.
- According to the U.S. Department of Energy, for every 5 miles an hour you drive over 60 mph, it's like spending an extra twenty cents per gallon of gas.
- Carrying around heavy loads reduces a car's gas mileage.
- Idling for longer than a minute or two actually uses more gas than starting the car, except in the case of hybrids.
- Properly maintained engines operate more efficiently and get better gas mileage.
- Properly inflated tires improve mileage and are safer to drive on.

THE CHOICES YOU CAN MAKE . . . **WHEN GETTING FROM HERE TO THERE**

CHAPTER 9
The choices you can make . . .
WHEN EATING

149 Learn to Eat Green

The organic food market has grown by leaps and bounds over the past decade. Where organic food was once limited to specialty stores and markets, it's now available almost everywhere. Even Wal-Mart is getting in on the trend, looking to double the number of organic products they sell in the near future. Organic food has even become an important part of restaurants, and food services are being revamped in school cafeterias and corporate lunch counters across the country.

150 Understand Organic

The definition of organic varies depending on who is involved in the conversation. Generally, organic refers to the growing, raising, or processing of food without drugs, synthetic chemicals, or hormones using methods that conserve natural resources and limit the effects on the environment. But how do you know if something is really organic? As organic food increased in popularity, consumers began calling for the standardization of the organic labeling process to ensure that important criteria were met before a label could be obtained.

151 Know the Lingo

The Organic Foods Production Act of 1990 helped create the National Organic Program (NOP), which is run through the U.S. Department of Agriculture (USDA). The NOP prepared standards, the National Organic Program Regulations, and all organic certifiers were required to be in compliance with these regulations by the end of 2002. Foods meeting the USDA requirements for being organic will have a USDA seal. To obtain the seal, foods must be 95 percent organic. Foods using only organic products and methods may also

THE CHOICES YOU CAN MAKE . . . **WHEN EATING**

state "100% organic" on the packaging. A lower level of organic certification is available for foods that are 70 to 95 percent organic. These foods can be labeled as "made with organic ingredients."

152 Clarify Organic Certification

To obtain the organic certification, farmers must find a certification agent through either a state or private agency. They must complete an application, documenting information such as pest management practices, seed and seedling sources, storage and handling measures, and monitoring practices. The agent certifies the paperwork and assigns an organic inspector to review operations at the farm. If everything is in place, the certification agent will approve organic certification and the farm can use the organic label.

153 Shop 'till You Drop

According to the Organic Trade Association, the sale of organic foods increased 16 percent in 2005 alone, bringing in $13.8 million in sales. More and more fresh, whole food, and organic grocers are popping up across the United States, and traditional grocers and food producers are starting to taking notice. For example, Whole Foods Market started in Austin, Texas, and now operates more than 200 stores in the United States, Canada, and the United Kingdom. Not only are they the world's leading retailer of natural and organic food, *Fortune* magazine consistently lists Whole Foods as one of its top 100 companies to work for. Whole Foods came in at number five in the 2007 list.

154 Believe It—Brand Name Organics

Feeling pressure from growing specialty organic stores, more mainstream grocery stores are including a variety of organic food in their inventories as well. Brands such as Nature's Best and Newman's Own are common in many conventional grocery stores. Many stores have even started their own lines of organic foods. The Kroger Company, the country's largest supermarket, started the Naturally Preferred line in 2002, which now includes more than 275 items. Even large food producers are getting in on the organic options. Kraft Foods now makes USDA-certified organic macaroni and cheese, and their DiGiorno spinach and garlic thin-crust pizza is made using organic ingredients.

155 Shop at Small Grocers

Most people are used to having a variety of fruits and vegetables available year-round. But for this to happen, fruits and vegetables have to be trucked and transported, which causes the increased consumption of fuel and produces carbon dioxide. Smaller independent markets buy locally grown fruits and vegetables that are fresh and seasonal. That means the produce you eat spends more time ripening on the vine than traveling across the country—or the world. A growing movement encourages food labels to include information about how many miles the product traveled from the farm to the store. This information would allow shoppers to purchase more locally grown produce and avoid food that's made a longer haul.

156 Consider Going Vegetarian or Vegan

Vegetarianism—a lifestyle based on a choice not to consume meat, fish, or poultry—has been practiced for thousands of years. The choice can be based on health, religion, or personal preference, but the well being of the environment has become another reason to embrace vegetarianism in recent years. Being a vegetarian does not automatically exclude dairy products or eggs from the diet; that's an individual choice. Vegans are a stricter form of vegetarians. They eat no animal flesh or products and abstain from wearing or using animal products such as leather, silk, wool, lanolin, or gelatin. Then there are dietary vegans who adhere to a strict diet but are amenable to using animal products.

157 Eat for Your Environment

There are a variety of reasons beyond concern for the environment to adopt a vegetarian lifestyle. The quality of life for livestock can be an influential factor. Rather than allowing cows and other animals to graze and forage naturally, they are confined and fed grain and corn grown using pesticides and transported to farms by truck and over rail. Overall, the meat consumes massive amounts of energy, burdening the soil, groundwater, surface water, and air. Health is another reason to give up meat and meat products. Forgoing, or even reducing, meat consumption can lower cholesterol and limit the intake of unnecessary chemicals such as hormones and antibiotics.

158 Think about Fish

Fish can be a good source of protein without the saturated fats in other meats. Fish also contain essential vitamins, minerals, and omega-3 fatty acids, which have been shown to prevent heart disease and may even help brain development. Many fish are caught in the wild; others such as salmon are frequently farm raised. Many people in the seafood industry understand that their livelihood depends on sustaining the fish population decades into the future, but some populations are in danger of overfishing. Overfishing decreases a population to the point where it cannot replenish itself through natural breeding. This has serious repercussions for the entire ecosystem as species are depleted and are unable to fulfill their traditional roles as predator or prey.

159 Watch Your Mercury Consumption

Mercury is a naturally occurring element. Unfortunately, it is also released into the air by industrial pollution such as waste incinerators. When mercury falls in streams and oceans, bacteria chemically changes some of it to methylmercury, which is absorbed by fish as they feed. The methylmercury is then stored in the tissues. The amount accumulates over time, so older and larger fish are more likely to have higher levels of mercury. Fish that are higher up on the food chain also tend to accumulate more mercury than their prey. Certain people, particularly pregnant women and small children, are advised to stay away from fish with high levels of mercury, such as shark, swordfish, king mackerel, and tilefish. Mercury hinders neural development, and fetuses, infants, and small children are especially susceptible. More information on the advisory can be found at *www.epa.gov/waterscience/fishadvice*.

160 Follow the Recommendations from an Aquarium

The Monterey Bay Aquarium in California takes an active role in educating people on current fishing techniques and better selection of sustainable seafood. The organization offers the following recommendations for consumers and fishermen:

- Whether in a store or restaurant, ask where the fish came from and how it was caught. You might also have the option of ordering local.
- Opt for oysters, scallops, squid, and clams over grouper, tuna, and shark.
- Don't discard fishing gear in the water. Tangled lines and hooks can hurt or kill marine life such as turtles and sea birds.
- Don't fish in protected areas, which allow exhausted fish populations to recover. By staying away from them, you can support replenishment of the species.

- Put down that seashell the next time you're tempted to bring it home. It's important that people avoid taking certain seashells from the beach or purchasing them from tourist shops and craft stores. In fact, enclosed or "conch" shells are often homes to sea life that depend on them for protection.

161 Reconsider Animals Raised as Food

Organically raised meat is becoming more commonplace, with companies like Coleman Natural Products, the largest natural meat company in the United States, selling its products at more than 1,650 stores nationwide. Maverick Ranch Natural Meats, for example, offers a line of meats including beef, chicken, turkey, pork, lamb, and buffalo. Owned by the Moore family, they allow their cattle to forage and graze in pastures free of pesticides. They also refrain from the use of steroids and antibiotics. The animals are all "Certified Humane Raised and Handled" by Humane Farm Animal Care, a nonprofit organization that works to ensure farm animal welfare. Cows, poultry, and pigs raised using conventional methods, however, are all fed unnatural diets that include hormones and antibiotics. These additives help the animals reach their slaughter weight more quickly and decrease disease in animals kept in close quarters. There is concern that animals' bodies do not completely break down the hormones, allowing them to enter the environment through manure and wastewater.

162 Avoid Genetically Modified Foods

Objections to the use of genetically modified foods include both environmental and health concerns. It is unsure if plants that are genetically modified for pest resistance could harm unintended and desirable insects. There is also concern that target insects could actually become immune to the pesticides. Environmental concerns include the potential for engineered crops to crossbreed with weeds. Altering crops to resist herbicides could result in mighty weeds undeterred by herbicides. Health concerns include the potential for allergens to be introduced as part of the genetic modification, causing dangerous reactions in some people. Overall, many people are concerned with the unknown effects genetically modified food could have on their health.

163 Know What's in Your Dinner

Processed food is likely to contain food additives. Additives help extend the life of some foods, add nutrition, or change a food's consistency. Some additives are relatively straightforward, and by reading the label, you will know what has been added. Some, however, are less conspicuous. Of course, this is of particular concern if you have allergies or are trying to avoid certain foods such as meat. If you are unsure whether the listed ingredient on a package is or contains an allergen, contact the manufacturer using the contact information on the product.

164 Eat Out Green

Patronizing green restaurants means supporting businesses that incorporate sustainable business practices in their operations; some green restaurants serve only organic or natural food as well. Restaurants with green operations conserve energy by using Energy Star appliances and low-flow spray nozzles and by reducing, reusing, and recycling materials such as cardboard, plastics, and glass. They prevent pollution by making sure that grease traps are cleaned and that biodegradable soaps are used for cleaning. The Green Restaurant Association certifies restaurants, coffee shops, and college and university cafeterias that operate in sustainable ways. Information on their certification process can be found at *www.dinegreen.com*.

165 Do a Bit of Research, Make a Difference

Local Harvest (*www.localharvest.org*) is an organization that keeps a directory of restaurants, farmers' markets, cooperatives, and farms that use sustainable practices and organic products. Their database covers the entire United States and includes products ranging from flowers to beef. Consumers wield power with their wallets, so when dining out, ask questions about the food. For example, many of the fish served at restaurants are not recommended for consumption either because of mercury concentrations or overfishing. The server may not likely know the answers to all the questions, but the management probably does. For larger chain restaurants, consider contacting members of the board with your concerns about the food they serve.

166 In Your Own Kitchen, Abide by These Rules

Conserving energy is a big part of reducing your impact on the planet. Some ways to conserve energy in the kitchen include using as small an oven as possible. The larger the oven, the more energy it takes to heat it to the proper temperature. Glass and ceramic retain heat better than metal; switching will reduce the temperature as much as 25 degrees. When using the stove, make sure the burner fits the pan; an uncovered burner wastes heat. And always use a lid when heating items on the stove for the same reason.

CHAPTER 10

The choices you can make . . .

WHEN DRINKING

167 Watch What You Ingest

Some drinks start as fruits on trees, some as leafy plants on the ground, while others course through limestone below the ground. The most important beverage, of all, is water. Without it, people have only days to live. It's a lubricant. It regulates metabolism and controls body temperature. It moves things around, from joints to food through the digestive system. It's calorie-free and readily available at almost everyone's fingertips. It's important to consider what we drink as part of green lifestyle decision-making.

168 Look Deeper—What's in Your Water?

Bottling companies rarely put the source of the water on the bottle. That's because chances are it didn't come from the clear running stream shown on the label. The labels do include contact information for the company, so you can call to find out the source of your bottled water. Unless you are traveling in an area where the water isn't safe to drink, there's no need to avoid the tap. Public water supplies are regulated and, by law, are required to be tested regularly. Bottled water, although it's been found to be safe, isn't required to meet the same criteria as public water supplies.

169 Avoid Bottled Water

The business of delivering millions of gallons of water in separate bottles is incredibly inefficient. Rather than taking advantage of existing treatment and distribution systems, bottlers individually package their water and ship it across the country. Plastic bottles are made from petroleum, and trucking them across country uses a lot of gas. The surge in bottled water has left mountains of plastic in its wake. Plastic bottles can be recycled for use in a variety of products, from other bottles to carpet, but some inevitably end up in landfills and incinerators all over the country.

170 Recycle Those Bottles

According to the Container Recycling Institute, if people recycled 70 percent of the bottles they purchased for one year, greenhouse gases could be reduced by 20,000 metric tons of carbon equivalent. It would also save the equivalent of 600,000 barrels of crude oil needing to be extracted and processed. Currently only eleven states have bottle bills that require refund systems for returning used water bottles. Companies that purchase recycled bottles for use in manufacturing prefer to buy plastics from states with bottle bills. The streams from these states contain only plastic bottles, making them much easier to use because additional sorting isn't necessary.

171 Wash and Reuse Your Bottles

There has been quite a bit of debate lately over whether people should reuse single-use water bottles or toss them out. One concern is whether the bottles can be adequately cleaned to remove bacteria. Disposable bottles have narrow necks that make washing them nearly impossible. Bacteria from people's hands and mouths make their way into the bottles where they can make people sick. So after you've emptied it, clean your bottle with hot soapy water, making sure to get around the neck of the bottle. Let your bottle air-dry. To keep from contaminating your water bottle with germs, wash and dry your hands before you refill it, and make sure you're the only one using your water bottle.

172 Beware of Number Three

Another concern about reusing single-use bottles is that the chemicals may be released during the washing process. The primary concern is phthalates, which are added to some plastic to keep it flexible so it won't crack. Phthalates, the most common being di (2-ehtylhexyl) phthalate, are suspected to be endocrine disruptors that

THE CHOICES YOU CAN MAKE . . . **WHEN DRINKING**

interfere with reproductive organs of both males and females. The FDA has approved of the use phthalates in plastics that are used to produce food and drink containers, but other agencies such as the National Institute of Environmental Health (NIEH) and the Center for Disease Control (CDC) are concerned about the potential impacts of phthalates in plastic. Avoid water bottles with the recycle number three in the triangle on the bottom of the bottle. Water bottles with the recycle numbers one and two are considered safe.

173 Rethink Soda

Soda consumption has skyrocketed over the past five years, increasing 500 percent. Soft drinks make up approximately 28 percent of all drinks consumed. But soda may not be such a good choice when it comes to options regarding people or the planet. The good news is, the move to organics hasn't only affected food; it's made a difference in the beverage industry, too. If you need to have that fizz when it comes to drinks, there are some organic and healthy options to choose from. Blue Sky Beverage Company (*www.drinkbluesky.com*) offers a line of organic sodas made with all natural ingredients and no preservatives or artificial colors. Santa Cruz Natural (*www.scojuice.com*) makes organic fruit juice sodas in flavors such as ginger ale, root beer, lemon lime, and vanilla crème. R.W. Knudson (*www.knudsenjuices.com*) makes fruit spritzers in flavors such as black cherry, mango, and tangerine.

174 Fake Your Fizz Fix

You can also look to club soda or seltzer water. Seltzer water is filtered water that's been carbonated. Club soda is water that's had minerals and mineral salts added to it; just be careful to watch the sodium content. The Healthy Beverage Company (*www.steaz.com*), makers of Steaz Green Tea Soda, now offers Steaz Energy, the first energy drink that has been USDA organic and fair trade certified. It's made from tea that's Fair Trade Certified and includes a caffeine kick not just from green tea but from Guayaki yerba mate. The yerba mate tree is native to South American rain forests that have been heavily damaged by deforestation. It's hoped that conscientious farming of the yerba mate will help sustain the rain forest.

175 Milk It for All It's Worth

Of all the drinks consumed, milk comes in at third place, with more than 10 percent of the beverage market. But milk is more controversial than most people realize. The benefit of milk is that it is a primary source of calcium and vitamin D. A one-cup serving—eight ounces—supplies 30 percent of the daily recommended amount of calcium and 25 percent of vitamin D. It also contains significant amounts of protein, potassium, vitamin A, vitamin B_{12}, riboflavin, niacin, and phosphorus. So, yes, milk is good for us, but it is hard to make. In fact, cows in large numbers are quite a burden on the planet. A satiated dairy cow can produce 120 pounds of manure a day, and cows account for 28 percent of global emissions of methane, a greenhouse gas.

176 Milk Is a Tricky Business

Like most businesses, dairy farmers are under increased pressure to maintain profits even when operational costs rise and the cost of milk stays level. Dairy farms generally operate in one of two ways, either using grazing or non-grazing methods to feed the cows. Cows living on factory farms, those that are non-grazers, expend little energy on anything other than producing milk. Their food is brought to them and they don't move much. The reason pasture cows, the ones that do graze, make less milk than confined cows is that they spend energy walking from paddock to paddock. In short, pasture

THE CHOICES YOU CAN MAKE . . . **WHEN DRINKING**

cows spend more time being cows. Research, studies, and evaluations abound regarding the profitability of both forms of farming. Both methods of dairy farming require daily milking of cows, and cows are slaughtered for meat when their milking days are over.

177 Go Organic

Many dairy cows are given bovine growth hormones (BGH) to encourage milk production and antibiotics to ward off infection. Organic milk, which comes from cows that have been given neither, has increased in popularity as people become more aware of the antibiotics and hormones given to cows. However, the United States Department of Agriculture (USDA) is working to define clearly what constitutes organic milk. Although the USDA understands that organic milk should come from cows that have not been subjected to growth hormones or antibiotics, the use of pasture or confinement farming has not been well defined. Many organic farmers do allow pasture grazing for their dairy.

178 Avoid Growth Hormones

Two New England farms that have made the switch to organic include Dean Foods and H. P. Hood. These two dairies started by eliminating the use of artificial growth hormones. It is the farms' hope that this step will alleviate consumer concerns without dramatically increasing the cost of the milk. It's expected that the hormone-free milk can be offered at half the price of organic milk.

179 Consider a Milk Alternative

If you are planning to subtract dairy products from your diet, then soy, rice, or almond milk can be good replacements for cow's milk. These substitutes are extracted from natural ingredients that do not produce manure or methane, two environmental detriments for which cows are responsible. Like organic milk from cows, these alternatives also allow you to avoid hormones associated with the dairy industry. In addition, since a primary component of a cow's diet is plants, by drinking milk made from plants, you are bypassing the animals all together and getting your nutrients straight from the source. Additionally, soy and almond milk actually contain comparable amounts of protein when compared to dairy, with rice coming in slightly behind. Nutrients not present in dairy alternatives such as calcium, vitamin D, vitamin B_{12}, and riboflavin are usually added. Not all milk products taste the same so it may be worth trying a few different brands. Once relegated strictly to health-food stores, you can now find a variety of nondairy milk products in many chain grocery stores.

180 Take a Closer Look at That Cup of Coffee

There are some things to think about as the coffee makes its way to the grinder, the brewer, and then into a cup. The environment suffers at the expense of coffee's popularity. Often, when land is cleared and coffee trees are planted, pesticides and fertilizers are needed to support an increasing demand. Some organizations combat this by encouraging shade-grown coffee, where trees are either planted within the existing forests or other plants, like fruit trees, are incorporated into the planting. Fewer fertilizers and pesticides are needed with this method. The shade provided by the trees protects the plants from direct sun and rain and helps maintain soil quality. This means fewer weeds, reducing the need for fertilizers and herbicides. The shade also provides homes for birds that feed on insects, eliminating the need for pesticides. When the natural forest is left intact, migratory birds and other native species are impacted less.

181 Let's Talk about "Green" Tea

Organizations such as the USDA and the Organic Trade Association encourage environmentally friendly methods of growing tea. Incorporating nature into the growing process can help avoid the need for pesticides, herbicides, and synthetic fertilizers. Using compost and natural organic matter can deter weeds. Crop rotation and mulching can encourage spider and earthworm populations that are helpful in destroying harmful insects and in optimizing soil quality.

182 Switch to Organic Juice

Orange juice can be green. Before gulping down your juice on the way out the door, consider where it came from and how it got to the table. Pesticides have been used to protect crops, but organic companies are leading the charge toward less pesticide use. Organic fruit juice generally relies on family farms to provide the needed fruits and vegetables.

183 Try Organic Wines

When it comes to the environment, many wines have become or are working toward a certified organic designation. The National Organic Program (NOP) is part of the USDA and has set guidelines for whether items can carry the organic label. The NOP has determined levels of organic conditions and processing for wines so consumers can chose how organic they want to go when it comes to raising a wineglass. For a wine to be labeled "100% organic," the grapes must have been grown in completely organic conditions and sulfites must not have been added. If a wine is made from 95 percent organic ingredients and has no added sulfites, it can post the "organic" label. Naturally occurring sulfites must not exceed a concentration of 100 parts per billion. Wines can also boast that they are made with organic ingredients. To do this, they must contain a minimum of 70 percent organic ingredients. To hold the title, the label must include a list of the organic ingredients. Organic wines are available at a variety of liquor stores and wine shops.

184 Drink Green Beer

The organic beer label means that the barley, hops, and other ingredients are grown and processed without pesticides, fungicides, and fertilizers. Organic beer can be purchased at many stores, especially those catering to whole and organic foods. If you are looking for a local brewery, visit *www.beertown.org* and use the brewery locator. Many local microbreweries and vintages make organic beers and wines. By buying locally, you reduce the travel miles associated with getting the drinks from farm to market. If you're feeling particularly bold, home brewing and wine making is also an option. Organic ingredients can be purchased at local farmers' markets and grocery stores. If you are interested in learning more about home brewing, check out the Seven Bridges Cooperative at *www.breworganic.com*.

CHAPTER 11

The choices you can make . . .

WHEN RECYCLING

185 Look at Yourself as a Consumer

Spending has been encouraged for generations as a way to measure success and even to show affection. Being a good consumer is generally defined as being a buyer, pumping money into the economy. Your patronage generates a need for services and manufacturing, which creates jobs and benefits everyone. But there can be a downside to consumerism, too. Many products are not manufactured with environmental responsibility in mind. As production goes up, so does its impact on the environment. This can be especially true if keeping costs low is the greatest factor in producing anything, from sweatshirts to picture frames.

186 Buy What You *Need*

You can make a difference. By choosing to eliminate some purchases, you can cut down on the amount of waste generated. It's been said that the world today is a throwaway society. But as the green movement progresses, this may change. When shopping, consider not just the quantity but the quality of what you buy. The cheapest product isn't always the best choice. Are you buying from conscientious companies? Were the products made from sustainable practices? Every purchase is a vote, and you as a consumer wield more power than you may think. Being a good consumer means thinking about the impact of what you buy, both economically and environmentally.

187 Support Green Businesses

Conscientious manufacturers keep the environment in mind when designing products and deciding how to package and transport them. Businesses can also modify their products and methods for more sustainable production. Sustainable business programs and practices are more prevalent in Europe and countries like Australia and New Zealand, but greener practices are starting to make headway in the United States as well. Sustainable, or green, businesses operate in ways that improve or minimize their damage to the environment. These companies work to integrate economic, environmental, and social considerations into the business network. Changes to business practices may have impacts as far-reaching as those of the Industrial Revolution.

188 Choose to Reduce

Until manufacturing has conquered the obstacles to successful sustainability, it's up to consumers to make educated decisions when purchasing products. Follow these general rules:

- Make a list and check it twice. Whether you're shopping for groceries, school supplies, makeup, or home repair items, sticking with a list will avoid unnecessary or impulse purchases.
- Avoid the just-in-case purchase. If you aren't sure you need something, just assume you don't. Being organized at home can help you know what you have in stock.
- Evaluate want versus need. Consider if a purchase is for something you need or want. If it's just a desire, can it be quelled?
- Beware of bargains. They're designed to move merchandise, not necessarily to save you money.
- Beware of warehouses. That twenty-five-pound bag of flour may seem like a good deal, but if it ends up getting thrown away, then it's not.
- Walk to the store. You'll buy only what you can comfortably carry.

189 Learn to Reuse

So many items have become or are made to be disposable that it's easy to forget that not everything has to be thrown away. Pack your peanut butter and jelly sandwich in a reusable container instead of plastic wrap. Carry the drink of your choice in a plastic bottle instead

THE CHOICES YOU CAN MAKE . . . **WHEN RECYCLING**

of relying on multiple one-use cups throughout the day. Reusing avoids the production of new items, and it also cuts down on the wasteful products you consume. It eliminates waste that in the end will likely be disposed of in a landfill or incinerated. Also, some cities and counties have collection centers where reusable materials can be collected and stored. Items like paint and motor oil are shelved and available for free to other residents. Most communities have turned to online swapping using sites such as *www.freecycle.org* and *www.freesharing.org*. These organizations allow items to be reused without having to maintain a storage unit. Members post what they have available, from paint to furniture to baby items, and other members scan the lists and ask for the items that they would like. The decision of who gets what is usually made based on the response time.

190 Follow This Reusable Check List

Reuse materials by taking small steps that can be incorporated into your life a little at a time. Here are a few for starters:

- Reuse totes and bags. When going to the grocery store or the mall, take along your own bags.
- Make a charitable donation. If you know of an organization in your area that's looking for household items, clothes, or even cell phones, consider making a donation.
- Be creative. Printer paper has two sides and can be reused as scrap paper. Packaging materials can be used for arts and crafts projects. Sunday comics make colorful wrapping paper.

191 Remember to Recycle, Too

Recycling started decades ago as container deposits. People collected glass bottles, returned them to stores, and traded them in for refunds. The bottles would be washed and put back on store shelves.

In the 1960s, aluminum cans became more prevalent; with drink bottles no longer being returned for money, litter began cluttering the roadside. In an effort to reduce pollution, some states passed bottle bills to encourage the return of glass and plastic bottles and aluminum cans. Eleven states have active bottle bills. Recycled materials have now become a part of the processing stream, taking the place of virgin materials in manufacturing. Manufacturing with recycled materials conserves raw materials and reduces energy consumption.

192 Be Part of the Recycling Loop

The recycling loop includes three steps: collecting recyclable materials, physically recycling the materials, and purchasing items made from recycled materials. As a first step, many communities have set up curbside recycling programs in which materials such as newspaper, plastic, and glass are collected in containers separate from waste. Some towns and cities that don't offer curbside pickup have recycling facilities where residents can drop off recyclable materials free of charge. It is simple to recycle at home. Keep the recycling containers in a convenient location, possibly in or close to the kitchen. You may not be consistent early on, but eventually recycling will become a habit that you incorporate into everyday tasks. Separating the recyclables is one of the most important factors when it comes to making recycling economical. After everything is sorted, it's compacted and baled and ready for sale.

193 Watch the Recycling Industry Boom

Today's recycling market is as sophisticated as any other business, with stocks traded and futures projected. Processes continue to evolve to provide better quality and more consistent sources of

THE CHOICES YOU CAN MAKE . . . **WHEN RECYCLING**

recycled materials, and manufacturing changes allow the use of recycled materials. As these trends continue, recycled products will become a viable and vital component of manufacturing. It's likely that with improved recycling processes and a consistent demand, recycled materials will become more economical. The three main recycled materials are plastics, metals, and paper, and each has its own markets and uses.

194 Get to Know Your Plastics

Plastic bottles are everywhere from the refrigerator to the laundry room, each with an arrowed triangle and number stamped on the bottom. The seven numbers associated with recycled plastic can be confusing, but each number represents what that product can be recycled into. From those plastic bottles comes everything from fiberfill for pillows and sleeping bags, to license-plate frames, to plastic lumber. Once sorted at the recycling facility, plastics are baled and sent out for processing. There the plastics are cleaned, possibly sorted by color, and converted to flakes and pellets. Then they're sold to manufacturers for use as feedstock.

195 Make Sense of the Metals Around You

Everything from aluminum soda cans to used engines can be recycled; it's just a matter of getting them sorted and to the right place. Currently, whole engines can be sent overseas to countries such as India and China where labor rates are low, and it pays to break down engines manually into separate components like copper wiring and steel casing for recycling. The same shipping companies that bring merchandise from China and India to the United States take back our recyclables. It's a cycle. When you recycle your metals, make sure to separate them appropriately so they go to the right place!

196 Get to Know Paper Specifics

Like other materials, paper is sorted and baled in the recycling facility. Bales of flattened cardboard and bales of mixed paper and newsprint are sold to mills for processing. Processing paper requires a progression of different treatments. When paper comes to the mill, it is pulped into fine pieces and water is added to make slurry. The slurry is run through a screen so pieces of glue and other contaminants can be removed. From there, the soupy mixture is cleaned by spinning it around in a cone-shaped cylinder that causes heavy objects like staples to fall out. The pulp mixture is then de-inked, or brightened. During this process, sticky inks are removed. The mixture is then bleached to remove any remaining color. The end result is paper pulp that is ready to be used for processing.

197 Wage War with E-Waste

One of the largest concerns of recycling today is managing electronic waste. E-waste includes cell phones, computers, televisions, VCRs, copiers, and fax machines—anything with a battery or a plug. While some of this equipment can be recycled or donated to charities, much of it is obsolete or broken. When taken to a landfill for disposal, e-waste takes up valuable room. Worse, it has the potential to release metals such as mercury and lead into the environment, although placing e-waste in a landfill is healthier for the environment than incineration. When incinerated, the plastics release dioxins into the air. The only national legislation regarding e-waste applies to cathode ray tubes (CRT) from computer and television monitors. This legislation states that CRT will not be considered solid waste when processed for recycling. This act saves recyclers from having to abide by strict sold waste regulations and keeps the waste from being considered hazardous. But because it only affects one

THE CHOICES YOU CAN MAKE . . . **WHEN RECYCLING**

component of the volume of e-waste generated, it doesn't really help the e-waste recycling industry as a whole.

198 Know Your State's E-Waste Regulations

Some states have enacted legislation to address the growing problem of e-waste and e-waste recycling. California, for example, assesses an advance recovery fee when electronics are purchased. The amount of the fee varies from $6 to $10, depending on the size of the product, and goes into an account that's used to pay collectors and recyclers. An important concern with the recycling of e-waste is that portions of waste that are generated in the United States are now shipped to China and India for recycling. This has huge transportation costs, financially and environmentally. However, as these countries become overburdened by waste and citizens rally for stronger environmental laws, it is expected that exporting e-waste from the United States will be limited.

199 Don't Forget to Recycle These

Some items take up relatively small portions of the waste stream but should be recycled nonetheless:

- Single-use and rechargeable batteries are accepted by some radio electronics and office stores.
- Carpet and padding can be used to make other carpet and padding. Ask when you're buying carpet if the old one will be recycled.
- Car parts such as batteries, used oil, and oil filters can usually be dropped off at local auto-part stores for no charge.
- Printer, fax, and inkjet cartridges can be recycled.
- Cell phones can be returned to your service provider to be reused or recycled.

- Some electronics stores will take your old materials for recycling. Call local stores to find out whether they will allow you to drop off your old electronics for recycling.

  For locations of other recycling organizations, see *www.earth911 .org.*

200 Think about Trash

When items that are no longer needed aren't reused or recycled, chances are they will end up in the trash. Just a generation ago, it was common to toss trash into sinkholes or spent mining pits or quarries, but now garbage is disposed of in highly engineered landfills or burned in incinerators. Federal legislation involving solid waste or garbage was initially enacted in 1966 and was born out of a need to protect human health more than the environment. Garbage was put in open dumps where pigs were allowed to scavenge and flies continued to breed. Much of the garbage was then burned with no real controls in place. The Resource Conservation and Recovery Act was passed in 1976 and amended in 1984. States are now obligated to enforce either federal regulations or more stringent local laws for managing garbage. All solid waste facilities, both landfills and incinerators, are permitted by state or federal agencies and are required to be operated according to the applicable laws.

201 Learn about Landfills

As waste decomposes in a landfill, it produces a liquid called leachate. The leachate drains through the waste and collects on a liner of plastic sheeting in the bottom of the landfill. Leachate is usually pumped to storage tanks at the landfill facility and is later either pumped or trucked to a wastewater treatment plant. Because little was known about what happened when waste degraded, older landfills were not required to have bottom liners, and the leachate migrated into the ground where it contaminated groundwater or surface water. Decomposition also produces methane, which is a dangerous greenhouse gas. Methane can be collected through piping and used to generate electricity; however, there is a limited time in landfill life when this is economically feasible because methane generation peaks and then decreases. Vents are constructed on top of landfills that go into the waste and allow the gas to either disperse into the air or be collected and burned. The size of the landfill and the volume of gas produced dictate how methane is handled.

202 Investigate Incinerators

About 14 percent of collected solid waste goes to incinerators where it's burned at very high temperatures, which destroys bacteria and certain chemicals. However, incineration also produces air contaminants such as nitrogen oxides, sulfur dioxides, mercury compounds, dioxins, and carbon dioxide. The composition of the waste incinerated affects the types and quantities of compounds emitted. Pollution equipment is required at all incinerators, but strict adherence to operations must be maintained for the incinerator and pollution equipment to work properly. Waste-to-energy plants generate power from garbage that is incinerated and use the heat to generate steam and produce electricity. Construction of these plants is very expensive, but as the cost of energy continues to rise and the space for new landfills becomes harder to find, these facilities may become a more popular disposal approach.

CHAPTER 12

The choices you can make . . .

WHEN PICKING OUT CLOTHING

203 Choose Sustainable Clothing

One of the largest manufacturing industries around, textiles is looking greener these days. There are more options available for choosing sustainable clothing that's environmentally responsible. Where Earth friendly clothing was once mild in color and design, today's designs incorporate bright colors with professional and trendy styles that blend in with the other garments strutting down the catwalk.

204 Consider Your Clothes on a Deeper Level

Clothing is a process that starts with either renewable or nonrenewable feedstock, which is treated and woven, dyed, and sewn to produce a piece of clothing. The clothing may have started out as a fossil fuel, or a cotton plant, with many workers and manufacturing and transportation processes along the way. Most synthetic threads such as polyester are made from petroleum, which is a nonrenewable resource that even during the refining process produces contaminants. Synthetic fabrics and clothing are durable and relatively non-destructible, which means they don't easily degrade. And when it comes to athletic clothing and sportswear, synthetic and synthetic blends that wick away moisture are hard to beat. Some companies such as Patagonia accept used synthetic clothing for reuse as feedstock in their new synthetic blend fabrics. Wear these clothes and you won't have to do so much laundry!

205 Avoid Dry Cleaning

Once clothes are in your closet, how you wash and care for them impacts the environment, too. This is particularly true of dry cleaning. The traditional dry-cleaning process uses solvents with a little water to remove soil from dirty clothes. The solvent most often used is perchloroethylene, which is known in the industry as perc. There are green alternatives to dry cleaning today, including using carbon dioxide, the same gas that makes soda fizzy, under high pressure to clean clothes. Another alternative is GreenEarth (GE) Cleaning. Because the cleaning system relies on biodegradable silicone-based solvents, harmful chemicals don't linger on your clothes or in the environment. GE facilities can be found at *www.greenearthcleaning.com*.

206 Consider Your Clothes and the Use of Pesticides

As with many other crops grown using conventional methods, pesticides are used to kill insects before they can cause damage in cotton production. But to avoid the problems associated with pesticides, researchers have found a way to genetically modify cotton plants to be pest-resistant. Skeptics, however, do not believe the increased production will last and that nature will find a way around the resistant cotton, eventually making stronger pesticides necessary.

207 Wear an Organic Wardrobe

Organic cotton requires farmers to forgo using genetically modified seeds, chemical pesticides, and fertilizers. By going organic, the farmers no longer have to pay for expensive pesticides and receive a higher dollar value for their crop, sometimes bringing in twice as much. Organic cotton is a win-win situation for both the environment and the farmer. Organic cotton farmers often use ladybugs and other natural enemies to combat pests. Pests are also handpicked from the plants. While this process takes much more time than applying chemicals, the farmers make up for it with the high prices they receive for their crops. Another important factor is that by eliminating pesticides from crops, workers are no longer exposed to dangerous chemicals.

208 Use Hemp—as Others Have Throughout History

Hemp, the nondrug form of cannabis, suffers from its association with marijuana. However, it is environmentally friendly. It does not require pesticides, and because the plants grow so densely, herbicides are not required either. The hemp used in clothing is chemically different from the cannabis people smoke. The amount of the chemical responsible for making people high, THC, is much lower in industrial hemp. Hemp is available in a variety of clothing from T-shirts to sport jackets.

209 Consider Organic Wool

Wool is a renewable and sustainable fabric, but problems abound with conventionally grown wool. On the other hand, organically raised sheep live in pastures without pesticides and are not dipped in vats of chemicals. Healthy sheep are able to fend off parasites, making dipping unnecessary. Organic wool yarn is not chemically treated but washed using biodegradable soap. While some people may be allergic to lanolin, oil that naturally occurs in wool, wool in itself is non-allergenic. It's also naturally fire retardant, making it safer than treated clothing. Natural wool clothing is breathable but makes for a good insulator. It's durable and wrinkle resistant and can be dyed and spun into a variety of fabrics.

210 Find a New Use for Bamboo

Bamboo is a quick-growing grass. It's been known to grow several inches in one day. Two of the more redeeming qualities include that it removes dangerous carbon dioxide from the air as part of photosynthesis and that it can be harvested relatively quickly, meaning smaller amounts of land are needed to grow it. Bamboo doesn't require fertilizers or pesticides and is hypoallergenic. And to date, there hasn't been any genetically modified bamboo used in the apparel process. The fiber produced from bamboo is moisture wicking and antimicrobial. Clothing made from bamboo is colorfast and can be washed as if it were cotton clothing.

211 Splurge on Silk—a Renewable Resource

Silk is a protein fiber spun by moth larvae. It can be considered a renewable resource and is biodegradable; however, traditional harvesting and processing methods don't comply with everyone's idea of planet friendly. The majority of silk in the United States comes from China, Korea, Japan, and India. A limited number of companies offer silk while working to improve one or more aspects of the harvesting process. Both Peace Silk and Ahimsa Peace Silk allow the larvae to continue to grow inside the cocoons, requiring the threads broken by the moth's emergence to be spun back together. Christoph Fritzsch, a German company, offers organic silk and claims to use only silk from harvesters that employ good working conditions. The company also uses wind and other alternative power in its processing facility.

212 Understand the Process—Fiber into Fabric

Fibers from both natural and human-made materials are made into fabric at mills. Cooperatives like the Organic Exchange work with brands, retailers, and farmers to match organic fibers with mills and brands. To be certified organic, a mill must be cleaned of residues. If a farmer's crop is small, a mill won't stop work to clean the equipment, and independent farmers have difficulty finding mills. By working with cooperatives, farmers are able to combine their volume, making it more profitable for the mills to process their cotton. The farmers then have a better chance of selling their crops. Also, more and more brands are incorporating organic fiber lines and working with organic farmers to purchase their feedstock.

213 Watch Manufactures Who Make the Right Moves

Clothing manufacturers can help the environment by implementing sustainable designs and operations. By working toward using renewable energy and increasing energy efficiency, achieving improved health and safety for employees and the public, and addressing waste disposal and reclamation within the manufacturing process, companies can positively impact their neighborhoods and surrounding communities. The Institute for Market Transformation to Sustainability developed the Unified Sustainable Textile Standard specific to the garment industry for monitoring both social and environmental impacts through the life cycle of a garment. One area specifically addressed encourages manufacturers to reduce emissions.

214 Broadcast Your Message with Your Clothing

Because clothes send a message, no one has to leave anything to interpretation. You can wear a slogan and support an eco-friendly lifestyle or let the world know how you feel about politics or the environment. Chances are shirts printed with an environmental message will come from organically grown cotton and will not have been made in sweatshops. There are plenty of stores to check out online. If you are the creative type, you can purchase T-shirts wholesale and have your own message printed. T-shirt manufacturers have lines of organic T-shirts and will print slogans with little or no minimum order. Here's your chance to become an eco-entrepreneur or just give friends and family a gift with a conscience.

215 Give Those Clothes Away

Donating clothes to a charity or selling them to a conscription shop ensures that your materials are not unnecessarily wasted in a landfill. More and more manufacturers are turning to reusable or recycled materials for their clothing. On the flip side, there's no better to way to save resources than to buy clothes someone else isn't wearing anymore. It saves natural resources both in creating the material and processing it. The work has been done and the energy spent.

Consignment shops all over the country sell gently used clothing and accessories and can come in particularly handy when you need an outfit that you may only wear once or twice.

216 Recycle Clothing—It's Easier than You Think

Rather than recycling the whole garment, many items can be recycled for parts. An old pair of jeans can be sacrificed for parts to save other pairs, a patch here, a pocket there. Denim and other fabrics can also be kept for other homemade projects such as purses, pillows, and blankets. Old T-shirts from concerts or sport teams can be patched together to make a memorable quilt. Manufacturers are also incorporating recycling activities, using clothing that is no longer used, post-consumer waste, and material waste from processing, also known as postindustrial waste.

217 Recycle Your Shoes

Just as you have choices in buying clothing, you face similar decisions when it comes to purchasing shoes. Shoe manufacturing is heavily dependent on dyes, glues, chemically tanned leather, and rubber. The industry as a whole has been slow to incorporate more sustainable practices and improve environmental welfare. In 1993, Nike developed the Re-Use a Shoe program, which collects used athletic shoes and defective products. The shoes are accepted all over the world (locations are posted on their Web site at *www.nike.com*) and processed at recycling centers in China, Indonesia, and Vietnam.

218 Get to Know What's in Your Soles

Processing rubber is extensive and includes compounding and mixing, milling and calendaring, extruding, coating, cooling and cutting, building, vulcanizing, and grinding. Each step in the process generates emissions, wastewater, and solid waste material. Heavy metals are a primary chemical component and waste product of making rubber. But it doesn't have to be that way; rubber can be obtained from sustainable practices. Sustainable practices take into account healthy harvesting of the trees and proper handling of wastes. As efficient processing methods expand, using recycled or reprocessed rubber is also becoming more common. In many instances, recycled rubber is used to make flip-flops and soles for sneakers.

219 Repair, Don't Re-Buy, Leather

Leather is largely garnered from factory farming of cows and pigs. The process used to transform the animals' skin into the leather sold in stores depends largely on a mix of harmful chemicals. When buying leather products, consider fair trade organizations that rely on free-range cattle and good working conditions for the people processing the hides. Extend the life of shoes by having them repaired rather than replaced. This supports a local business, and it saves natural resources.

220 Accessorize Smart

The purse, the wallet, the belt, and the jewelry—all of these can help make your outfit. Look for accessories, such as purses, that incorporate organic and recycled materials. When it comes to purchasing jewelry, consider the eco-friendly options. Organizations such as Global Exchange carry jewelry made of silver and other bright gemstones made by small organizations in an effort to promote sustainability. Another group, greenKarat, promotes the use of recycled gold.

CHAPTER 13

The choices you can make . . .

WHEN TAKING CARE OF YOURSELF

221 Select Natural Personal Care Products

The move to more natural personal care products has grown in leaps and bounds recently, giving conscientious consumers more products to choose from. From natural to organic, there is a lot to consider when selecting products for a daily regimen. In addition, don't forget trying to avoid excess or inefficient product packaging. It is possible to choose products that aren't harmful to the environment and still bring out your natural beauty.

222 Be Concerned about Chemicals

If you are interested in more environmentally friendly lotions, shampoos, makeup, and soap, you may want to look at the chemicals in the products you use every day. The Environmental Working Group (EWG) is a watchdog agency comprised of scientists, engineers, and policy experts who sift through scientific data in search of potential risks to people and the environment. The group works in a variety of different consumer and environmental protection areas, including the beauty industry. The EWG maintains *Skin Deep*, a report on the chemical ingredients of thousands of personal care products. The *Skin Deep* report can be found online at *www.ewg.org/reports/skindeep2*.

223 Pick Safer Products

Here is a list of things you can do to pick out safer personal care alternatives:

- Read the fine print on the labels.
- When it comes to soap, go mild. Strong soaps can remove natural moisturizers.
- Cut back on the fragrance to avoid allergic reactions.
- Don't go for dark hair dyes. They may contain coal tar ingredients.
- Avoid baby powder. It's not healthy for babies to breathe it.

- Avoid giving children under six fluoridated toothpaste.
- Lay off the nail polish to avoid exposure to toluene and acetone. If polish is used, make sure the area's well ventilated.
- Lighten up with the cologne. Many fragrances contain phthalates (endocrine disruptors) and parabens (chemicals linked to breast cancer).
- Try to cut back on the number of products used.
- And of course, use the lists on Skin Deep to find personal care products with minimal amounts of chemicals.

224 Think about Animal Testing

Although efforts have been made to reduce and eliminate animal testing, it is still the primary method of providing data on most cosmetics. Its continued use is partly based on the familiarity with the protocols and data analysis. Testing is performed both on finished products and individual ingredients. To find cruelty-free cosmetics, look for the leaping bunny logo. The leaping bunny symbol is awarded by the Coalition for Consumer Information on Cosmetics, an organization made up of eight national animal rights groups. The coalition works with companies to promote non-animal testing and is making progress in the United States and overseas. Their shopping guide is available online at *www.leapingbunny.org/shopping_guide.htm*.

225 Be Particular about Packaging

Look for products that use recycled content in their packaging. You can also recycle some packaging material. Conscientious companies are making efforts to cut down on the nonrecyclable materials they use and reduce the toxicity of the nonrecyclable materials they cannot avoid. If you would like a favorite product to come with less packaging or to come with recycled packaging, call the manufacturer.

Generally, products have a toll-free customer service telephone number printed on the outside of the package. If one of the company's competitors offers less packaging, make sure to mention that, too.

226 Look Beyond the Label

Natural and organic labels are everywhere on personal care products, from face cleansers to face masks and everything in between. But the labels may not tell the whole story. Products that are used in natural skin care usually include botanical extracts and essential oils, but that doesn't mean all the ingredients are natural. The USDA certifies organic food but not personal care items. That gives companies some leeway when it comes to labeling, making it difficult for consumers to know whether a product is natural or organic.

227 Go Organic

Beyond eliminating the production and use of chemicals, purchasing organic products supports organic farming, which is better for the environment. Here is a list of skin care lines that contain organic ingredients:

- Dr. Hauschka Skin Care (*www.drhauschka.com*) offers customers a holistic approach to skin care that relies on plant extracts to bring out a person's essential beauty.
- Juice Beauty (*www.juicebeauty.com*) carries a line of cleansers, toners, exfoliants, and moisturizers made from freshly squeezed organic juices.
- Kiss My Face (*www.kissmyface.com*) carries a line of 150 all-natural products that have eliminated the use of unnecessary chemicals.
- Nature's Gate (*www.natures-gate.com*) provides personal care products that are environmentally friendly, developed using

natural botanicals. Plus, the company sells all its products in recycled packaging.

- Noah's Naturals (*www.noahsnaturals.com*) is a product line sold exclusively by Wal-Mart. Their products are made from organic herbs, essential oils, plant oils, and emollients.

228 Avoid Allergens

Products that are labeled as hypoallergenic may still cause allergic reactions. Labels such as hypoallergenic and allergy tested are up to the manufacturer's discretion and don't have to meet specific regulatory criteria. It's up to consumers to determine what's really hypoallergenic. Finding the perfect products may take trial and error. If you have a particular concern, such as reddish or very sensitive skin, you can call the company to consult on the best choices to make. Sometimes this information is available on the Web sites, providing recommendations based on skin type.

229 Use Organic Shampoo, Too

Many companies that produce organic skin care products also carry hair care products. A benefit of organic shampoos and hair care products is the absence of synthetic surfactants. These chemicals can persist through wastewater treatment plants and septic systems to end up in ground and surface water.

230 Try These Products

Here are a few companies that sell environmentally friendly hair care products:

- Terressentials (*www.terressentials.com*) products are 100 percent natural and chemical-free with no detergent or synthetic fragrances.

THE CHOICES YOU CAN MAKE . . . **WHEN TAKING CARE OF YOURSELF**

- J. P. Durga (*www.jpdurga.com*) offers all-natural chemical- and petroleum-free hair care products.
- Aubrey Organics (*www.aubrey-organics.com*) was started more than forty years ago when Aubrey Hampton developed his natural hair care product line.
- California Baby (*www.californiababy.com*) offers a selection of natural and organic hair care and other products for babies, kids, and adults with sensitive skin.

Prices for organic and all-natural hair care products may be a little higher than for traditional products, but they are comparable to products sold in hair salons. Look for organic and natural hair care products at the grocery store or the local whole-food grocer.

231 Be Mindful of Your Makeup

Like hair care and other organic products, natural or organic makeup may cost a little more than at a conventional store, but costs are comparable to other specialty lines. Some natural or organic makeup might be found in health-food stores or whole-food grocers, but a larger variety is available online. Many of the natural makeup lines rely on powder foundations as opposed to liquid to avoid ingredients that are more likely to cause irritation.

232 Try This Makeup

Here's a sampling of Web sites that carry organic and natural makeup that are cruelty free:

- Burt's Bees (*www.burtsbees.com*) makes a variety of earth friendly products. Better yet, the packaging is earth friendly as well.
- The Alchemist's Apprentice (*www.alchemistsapprentice.com*) carries makeup that was developed especially for sensitive skin.
- Canary Cosmetics (*www.canarycosmetics.com*) carries a variety of makeup designed for sensitive skin.

- TheOrganicMake-UpCompany(*www.theorganicmakeupcompany*
  .com) is a Canadian company whose makeup is organic, and
  vegan, too.

233 Assess Those Aerosols

Much of the concern about using aerosols in products such as deodorants and hairsprays comes from the use of chlorofluorocarbons, or CFCs. First developed in the late 1920s, CFCs became widely used as coolants for refrigerators and air conditioners, cleaning agents for electronics, and propellants for aerosols. In the 1970s, scientists discovered that CFCs were eating away at the ozone layer, damaging its ability to protect earth from the sun's harmful rays. CFCs also trap heat in the atmosphere and contribute to global warming. Because of these concerns, the Environmental Protection Agency (EPA) banned the use of CFCs in aerosols in 1978. CFCs are being phased out under the Montreal Protocol, administered by the United Nations Environment Programme (UNEP). As part of the agreement, industrialized nations were required to stop using CFCs by January 1, 1996, with developing nations following suit by the year 2010. Today, 191 nations abide by the Montreal Protocol. If you are concerned with the chemicals present in your favorite product, you can check out the material safety data sheets (MSDS) at *www.householdproducts*
.nlm.nih.gov.

234 Handle Your Aerosols with Care

Aerosols produce a mist of fine particulate matter; that's one of the qualities that allows an even and light distribution on your hair or under your arm. Studies performed on hair stylists have not indicated any propensity to life-threatening diseases, but they were susceptible to skin irritations and minor breathing problems. Use aerosols in well-ventilated areas to avoid any health risks. Aerosol cans are made of steel that can be recycled. They should be emptied before they are placed in the recycle bin to avoid explosion.

235 Just for Women

Once a month, women of childbearing age menstruate, necessitating the use of boxes and boxes of tampons and sanitary napkins, which adds up to a lot of waste. If you are particularly concerned with the waste produced as part of having a period and are willing to add to your laundry load, consider trying reusable sanitary pads. Other options include the Keeper, made from latex, and the Moon Cup, made from silicone; these menstrual cups can hold up to one ounce of flow for up to twelve hours. If you are interested, check out these and other reusable menstrual options at sites like *www.naturalwoman.com* and *www.pandorapads.com*.

CHAPTER 14

The choices you can make . . .

WHEN TEACHING YOUR KIDS

236 Be a Good Example

Being a parent is a great opportunity to set a good example for future generations. What children learn growing up will stay with them the rest of their lives. Whether you are a parent, thinking about taking the plunge, or an important player in a child's life, you can leave a positive and lasting impression on a child and on the environment, too. Trying to lead a greener family life doesn't have to happen over-night. Parents can take a deep breath, tackle items or concerns one by one, and then get ready to improvise.

237 Consider Breastfeeding

Although many parents anguish over whether to feed their babies mother's milk or formula, this we know is true: Breastmilk is more environmentally friendly than formula. The production of formula depends on concentrated animal-feeding operations (CAFO) of dairy cows and miles and miles of petrochemically based transportation. It's true that some formulas are dairy-free and are based on dairy substitutes such as soy. While this eliminates the dependency on CAFOs, it's still a highly industrialized process. Plus, soy may not pro-vide all of the nutritional requirements needed by growing babies.

238 Make Your Own Baby Food

The first food babies usually get their lips around is cereal. You can purchase cereal in a box or make it at home. Homemade cereal is a little more time–consuming, but it can be made in batches and fro-zen for easy use later. From cereal, parents move on to feeding baby other foods such as vegetables, fruit, and yogurt. Making baby food at home eliminates the single-serve containers used to sell baby food and the environmental impacts from manufacturing and transport-ing all those little jars.

239 Do You Homework on Diapers

Which kinds of diapers are best for babies and the environment? Some children are allergic to the dyes and fragrances in disposable diapers. Others may be sensitive to cloth diapers if they aren't changed quickly after they're soiled or if the diapers aren't washed well between uses. It will take just a bit of time to determine what works for your baby, but consider all of the choices!

240 Consider the Damage Done with Disposable Diapers

Disposable diapers make up about 1.3 percent of all the solid waste going into landfills today, and they're full of human waste that contains germs and viruses. When cloth diapers are washed, the solids are flushed down the toilet and treated with other waste at a proper wastewater facility. Landfills are not designed specifically to handle biological waste; however, when operated correctly, all liquid draining from a landfill is collected and disposed of at a wastewater treatment plant. More than the contents of the diapers, the volume of diapers and the ability to reduce any component of the waste stream going into a landfill is the concern. If diapers are incinerated, the chlorine bleach they contain is converted to dioxin, which is another mark in the negative column for disposables.

241 Try a Compromise

Many parents compromise when it comes to diapering, using cloth diapers at home but opting for disposables when traveling and at night. Parents can buy biodegradable and even flushable disposable diapers and inserts that draw urine away from the baby and make dumping solids much easier. Check the packaging for more information. Disposable diapers are handy, but cloth diapers have come a long way over the years. Pins can be used but are no longer necessary.

Parents or caregivers can opt to use form-fitting covers with Velcro straps or all-in-one diapers that have Velcro straps right on the diapers. You can even buy organic cotton and hemp. Diaper covers come in cool designs, making cloth a fashion statement. For additional information on cloth diapers and other accessories, check out *www.clothdiaper.com*, *www.cottonbabies.com*, *www.mother-ease.com*, and *www.softclothbunz.com*.

242 Get Green Sleep

The same environmental standards that apply to adult mattresses also apply to crib mattresses. Most commercial mattresses today include fire-retardant chemicals that have been linked to health issues. While most studies indicate that the safety afforded by treating the fabric with fire retardants outweighs the concerns of chemical exposure, no long-term tests have been done to support this statement. For an environmentally friendly option, consider a natural and organic mattress. Not only are beds made from these materials better for the environment, they can be better for babies when it comes to what they breathe and how well they sleep. Natural and organic bedding is made from natural rubber or latex and organic cotton or wool.

243 Opt for Organic Bedding and Blankets

Organic wool is sheared from sheep that are raised without pesticides or hormones, and the sheep are allowed to forage for at least one-third of their food rather than spending their days in a feedlot. Because wool is an excellent temperature regulator and it has its own fire retardants as well, organic wool is a great option for your child's bedding. Also, organic cotton makes for great sheets and blankets. For some parents, going organic may be the best way to ensure that no chemicals were used in growing the cotton or manufacturing the sheets.

244 Size Up Green Strollers and Slings

Concerns with strollers and other baby items are that are that they are made using plastic and soft polyvinyl chloride (PVC) coverings. This a concern with babies chewing on the materials, and issues arise from the environmental impact of the manufacturing process. Slings and baby carriers come in all shapes, sizes, and patterns and allow parents to keep babies close while keeping their hands free. Some slings snuggle the baby right up to Mom or Dad's chest while others, usually those for older infants, are worn on the hips or on the back. For information on slings and carriers, check out these Web sites: *www.theslingstation.com*, *www.peppermint.com*, *www.onehotmama.com*, and *www.ergobaby.com*.

245 Pick Environmentally Friendly and Safe Toys

There has been a lot of concern over the materials used to make children's toys, particularly PVC plastics. Chemicals added to plastic to soften it include phthalates, which are considered a carcinogen by the EPA. Phthalates are also suspected as endocrine disrupters that can affect hormonal activities in laboratory animals. There is concern that children could absorb phthalates contained in the toys when chewing on them; however, studies have shown that the children do not chew the toys long enough for the chemicals to be absorbed. Safety regulations for toys sold in the United States are governed by the Federal Hazardous Substance Act and respective amendments, along with the 1969 Child Protection and Toy Safety Act. Regulations are enforced by the Consumer Product Safety Commission (CPSC) and recalls are made if a toy is deemed unsafe.

246 Take Family Field Trips

Field trips can be a great way to expose kids to the wonders of the environment firsthand. To get the most out of the excursion, the

THE CHOICES YOU CAN MAKE . . . **WHEN TEACHING YOUR KIDS**

location and length of a visit should be age-appropriate. Consider taking children to a science museum, particularly one that's geared at least partially toward a child's interest. Here children are allowed to see, touch, and even crawl on or climb through nature exhibits. The Florida Museum of Natural History (*www.flmnh.ufl.edu*) on the campus of the University of Florida is home to a life-size limestone cave. Children and parents can walk through it, looking at geologic formations and searching for bats and other animals. Many museums also offer docents who lead tours, telling stories and providing information.

247 Look at the Life Around You

Take a trip to a park and experience nature firsthand on a nature walk looking for bugs and other wildlife. Some parks are home to rocks and formations that offer their own learning experience. Some parks regularly offer ranger-led walks, or one can be scheduled ahead of time, that will point out what the park has to offer. Local farms offer another outing. Taking children out to pick local fruit can show them how food is grown and harvested. They will learn what grows in their region with respect to the seasons. Even a trip to the grocery store can be a learning experience if you point out the labels and talk about where the fruits and vegetables were grown.

248 Read Green

Reading is a big part of most children's lives, and books and magazines are a good way to interest children in the environment. Childsake offers lists of environmental and nature books for children, organizing them by category (*www.childsake.com*). Your local librarian may also have some suggestions. Magazines introduce kids to environmental topic in quick gulps. *Ranger Rick*, *Kids Discover*, and *National Geographic Kids* give children the opportunity to learn about all different aspects of the natural world around them and ways to take care of it. The Internet also offers an array of sites that teach environmental lessons. Many state and local regulatory agencies have pages expressly for children. The EPA sponsors the Environmental Kids Club at *www.epa.gov*.

249 Get Your Teens Involved

If teenagers want to experience the outdoors and learn about the environment, they can participate in a parks program. Some programs include helping maintain facilities or teaching and leading children, while others focus on adventure. The Yosemite National Institutes offer teens from eighth through twelfth grade sleep-away camps at different parks. At the Olympic Park Institute in Washington, students can participate in the Elwha River Project that includes five days of exploring the ecosystem. The Yosemite Institute in California offers twelve days of backpacking, rafting, and rock climbing. Campers also perform research that could lead to college credit. More information on these programs is available online at *www.yni.org*.

250 Buy Snacks in Bulk

Snacks now come in portion-controlled packages. Not only do single-portion packages cost a lot, they produce an excessive amount of waste as all of the single wrappers are tossed in the trash. So while grabbing a snack out of the pantry and heading out the door may be convenient, there are more environmentally friendly alternatives. You can buy snacks in bulk, or at least more than a single-serving container, and pack individual servings in reusable containers yourself.

251 Avoid Prepackaged Lunches

Many children take lunches that are completely prepackaged from drink to dessert. They produce a hefty amount of trash because nothing is reusable and much of the lunch often goes uneaten. Moreover, these lunches contain very little nutrition and a lot of fat and preservatives. When packing a child's lunch, use reusable containers and pack only what you think your child will eat.

252 Plan Arts and Crafts

Arts and crafts projects can be a perfect opportunity to experience and learn from nature while spending time together. For example, you can make homemade play dough from ingredients common in any home. Just combine the following ingredients:

3 cups flour
½ cup salt
3 tablespoons oil
1 cup water

This mixture can be divided and tinted with food coloring. Other more nature-oriented crafts include using treasures found in the yard or garden to make a collage or decorate a picture frame. Make a tape bracelet with the sticky side out and let your children inspect the yard for odds and ends they can stick to their wristband. It's a perfect opportunity learn about seeds, plants, and leaves.

253 Investigate Holistic Health-Care Alternatives

Your choice of pediatrician is important. Like other doctors, there are pediatricians who practice holistic medicine. These doctors have received medical degrees and have continued their education with holistic coursework. Holistic doctors use conventional medicines and immunizations, but they also consider the whole child and how he or she fits in the environment.

THE CHOICES YOU CAN MAKE . . . **WHEN TEACHING YOUR KIDS**

CHAPTER 15

The choices you can make . . .

WHEN GOING ON VACATION

254 Take Part in the Trend—Ecotourism

Ecotourism is a hot buzzword in the tourism industry. What makes a trip ecological, environmental, or green? The general rule of thumb is that ecotourism meets three goals. It helps sustain the environment, the economy, and the culture of the area visited. Unless those three criteria are met, it may not be considered full-fledge ecotourism. Ecotourism comes in many shapes and sizes, from adventure trips for the highly skilled and proficiently athletic to the more relaxing, softer trips for those looking to experience nature without breaking a sweat.

255 Get to Know the Ecotravel Lingo

Terms used in the ecotravel industry may be confusing. Not all types of travel afford the same kind of environmental benefits to local people that true ecotourism does. Here's a rundown of the most common terms used:

Adventure tourism is usually nature-oriented and involves some amount of risk, but not all trips require a specialized skill or the desire to rough it.

Geotourism usually centers on the geographic nature of the environment. Tourism helps to enhance the environment along with culture and overall well-being of local residents.

Nature-based tourism relies on the natural environment or settings to entice travelers. This could include jungle lodges as well as whale-watching cruise ships. These may or may not be environmentally friendly.

Sustainable tourism protects the environment, meaning that travel will continue in the area without destruction of habit or damage to resources. The area's integrity will be maintained for future travelers.

256 Travel Smart and Get More out of Your Trip

When done right, ecotourism can help preserve or even remediate a locale. Not only does tourism raise money, it increases awareness of native cultures and the environment, bringing to life images from magazines or television, adding touch, smell, and taste. It gives tourists a reason to protect an environment or a culture because they've seen it firsthand. When it comes to money, villages and communities rely on tourism so they don't have to turn to other sources of income such as mining, drilling, and foresting that degrade their resources. Properly run lodges and low-impact tours can support an economy, proving an alternative for inhabitants to earn a living. Tourists can't visit the rain forests of Costa Rica if the trees have been cut down for lumber, and the leather craftsmen can't survive without tourists visiting the Otavalo Market of the Andes Highlands and purchasing their wares.

257 Watch Out for . . .

Because of the increase in ecotourism, some unscrupulous guides, agents, or establishments will use the label for tourism that really doesn't meet the eco-criteria. This not only takes away from those valid guides promoting and relying on ecotourism, but not all adventure vacations, sustainable tours, or nature trips are 100 percent beneficial to the environment and the term could be used as a marketing ploy to generate ticket sales. First, almost all travel involves the use of cars, planes, cruise ships, or other vehicles that depend on fossil fuels. Although tourists would be hard-pressed to avoid any degrading practices, minimizing them is possible—it just takes some preplanning. Also, while large crowds may spend a lot of money, they have negative impacts that must be considered. Crowds can inhibit certain animal behavior such as breeding, and trash generated from tourists can be costly if handled properly or dangerous to the environment if not.

258 Follow the Ecotravel Rules

When abiding by the true spirit of ecotravel, there are rules tourists can live by to make sure they are promoting the conservation of cultures, economics, and the environment. Treat locations as you would your home. While you may not live there, others do.

Study up. To get the most of out travel, prepare for your trip before you leave home. Learn about your destination.

Spend locally. Whether for a tour guide, transportation, food, or souvenirs, purchases help the local community. There is the opportunity to impact the economy and learn the culture.

Take nothing but pictures; leave nothing but footprints. One small stone or shell may not seem like much, but repeated over and over again could leave a shore or stream barren. Leaving discards only means someone else will have to follow behind, picking up trash—or worse, it stays put.

Conserve natural resources. Don't be wasteful of a community's resources. Resources such as water, wood, and gasoline may be harder to get than you might think. Green hotels or smaller inns may create less environmental impact than a larger commercial lodge.

Be respectful. Tourists are visitors. Be respectful of the people who call your travel destinations home. Consider the clothes you wear and how you speak in public.

259 Take into Account the Different Ways to Go

Thanks to the Internet and local libraries, there are plenty of resources available to help plan a trip. Ask others who have visited the area what they liked most or what they would change if they traveled there again. See if they have any recommendations for must-do side trips. Also, consider contacting local guides or outfitters and ask questions. The International Ecotourism Society (TIES) works with the Rainforest Alliance, helping both tourists and tour operators with sustainable travel. The organizations provide information to travelers on how to be a green tourist and on the different travel opportunities available. Check out bulletin boards online where travelers can share information on different trips they have made. One example is *www.ecotravel.com.*

260 Use a Travel Agent

Because ecotravel has become so popular, many travel agents include it in the gamut of trips they offer. The Center on Ecotourism and Sustainable Development (*www.ecotourismcesd.org*) recommends the following online companies to find an eco-friendly travel agent:

- Solimar Travel, *www.solimartravel.com*
- Preferred Adventures Ltd., *www.preferredadventures.com*
- Eco-Resorts, *www.eco-resorts.com*
- Adventure Life, *www.adventurelife.com*
- GAP Adventures, *www.gapadventures.com*

261 Work on Vacation

If you are not one to kick back and relax, even during vacation, you may want to consider a working vacation. These vacations allow people to volunteer their time while experiencing another culture or environment. These trips could range from blazing trails and patrolling forests in national parks to recording whale migration patterns. They could be organized or sponsored by local churches, humanitarian groups, or volunteer networks that give people looking for the opportunity a chance to volunteer away from home. Some Web sites offer tips on how to raise money to pay for humanitarian or working trips, and chances are that friends and family may be willing to contribute, too. Additionally, because of the volunteer nature of the trip and the work performed, the costs of working vacations are usually tax-deductible.

262 Join a Group and Go Together

If you aren't up to planning your own trip and would like to take advantage of having an expert on hand, consider booking a trip with an environmental group. Groups like the Sierra Club and Nature Conservancy arrange trips all over the world. Trips usually include hiking, kayaking, horseback riding, and other activities and are led by expert guides who share information on the local environment and wildlife. Like any other group activity, there may not be a lot of extra room in the schedule or flexibility for deviation or side trips, but travelers, especially those new to the locale, benefit by being led by a professional who knows the area and how to get around it.

263 Look into a Retreat

If you are looking for a relaxing vacation, a retreat may fit the bill. Retreats are usually located in secluded areas. They can focus on themes such as all-women, yoga and meditation, or vegetarian cooking and (better yet) eating. They usually include workshops and educational classes. Some include menus and classes for body detoxification, to cleanse the toxins and stress from everyday life. Retreats like this might include fasting and fitness workouts as well as massage. Keep in mind that these vacations tend to cater more toward relaxation and rejuvenation rather than ecological or sustainable travel.

264 Go on Outdoor Adventures in Parks in America

National, state, and local parks abound in the United States. Parks have a lot to offer from overnight stays to hiking, biking, and even riding trails. Many parks offer educational programs and ranger-led tours. Some of the programs may have a fee, while many of the tours and fire ring sessions, where rangers gather visitors around a campfire and tell stories or give information about the park and its inhabitants, are free. Joining a tour or program allows visitors to learn more about the park and have a chance to meet other vacationers as well.

265 Get to Know the National Park Service

National parks allow visitors to witness some of the country's natural wonders, and they also protect watersheds and vital elements in biodiversity. Designation as a national park means that no mining or hunting can take place, and timber cannot be removed. The area is protected as a resource, which also makes them popular destination spots. There are areas protected within the National Park Service that are not duplicated anywhere else. A number of beautiful and solitary parks are relatively unknown, so do your research. Check out *www.nps.gov* for more information.

266 See the Yosemite Example Yourself

Yosemite National Park, which hosts more than 3 million visitors a year, became the first park system to actively pursue a reduction in personal cars. In 2005, the park began operating eighteen 40-foot diesel-electric hybrid buses, encouraging visitors to use the free bus system instead of their own vehicles. As a result, the Environmental and Energy Study Institute reported a 60 percent reduction in nitrogen oxide, a 90 percent reduction in particulate matter, a 70 percent reduction in noise—and an estimated 12,500 gallons of gas saved.

Now Yosemite isn't alone. Many other parks are taking the initiative to ameliorate damages to the environment brought on by their popularity.

267 Visit State Parks

State parks provide an intriguing alternative to other traditional vacation spots like amusement parks. Nature parks are less expensive than amusement parks, and they offer the opportunity to see a little of your own—or someone else's—backyard. Many state parks offer guided tours and even overnight outings. Many state parks have online reservations available that allow visitors to pick their sites and pay online. Schedule and program information are usually available online, so you can plan your stay to take advantage of all the park has to offer. To find parks in your state or a state you plan to visit, go to the state's Web site.

268 Reconsider Souvenirs

Before picking out a little souvenir to take home, consider how it was made and where it came from. If an animal product or natural resource was used to make the item, then it's better left on the shelf. The knickknack of interest may not even be from that area. For example, oftimes, shells sold at beaches in the United States are imported from places with less strict environmental laws. Don't pick your own souvenirs from the sea or land either. It's likely they'll end up being thrown away far from their home, so it's best that they're left at the beach.

269 Take in a Festival or Expo

Many cities, especially the larger ones, sponsor green festivals and expos. Exhibitors staffing booths answer questions and provide advice and firsthand information on building, construction materials, home design, transportation, gardening, home energy, and other interesting green topics. Most expos also offer classes or workshops on topics such as food choices and how the environment is affected by what people eat. They will likely have movies and political presentations along with a concert or party. You may even get to see an environmental celebrity promoting a cause. So when planning your vacation, be sure to check out festivals and expos at *www.green festivals.org* and *www.livinggreen.org*. Also visit the online version of the local newspaper to see what events are scheduled.

270 Sign Up for a Backyard Adventure

Staying close to home gives you the opportunity to get to know the animals that share your yard. If you like them, you can take steps to attract them. Find out what plants grow in your area that will attract birds and butterflies. To attract even more animals, plant a garden and see who comes to visit. Putting up a bird feeder and birdbath will attract feathered friends that are either local to the area or just passing through. Outdoor fans may be surprised to find out what kind of endangered species inhabit nearby areas. You can work to help sustain the animal populations. Even if long trips aren't possible, at-home ones may provide just as much fun and excitement.

271 Find Fun in Your City Park

Nearby city parks can also provide an opportunity to get closer to nature. Parks provide open space for locals to get fresh air and for children to run around and work out their wiggles. Trees help clean the air and provide habitat for birds and squirrels. They offer physical relief and visual respite, too. Green spaces break up the monotony of structures and roads and offer people a chance to take a breather.

There's a chance that local parks and recreation departments are in need of volunteers. By helping park professionals, volunteers are able to learn a lot about their surroundings and the issues they face, from funding to encroachment.

CHAPTER 16

The choices you can make ...

WHEN CARING FOR YOUR PET

272 Learn to Care for Pets

Domesticated animals play an important role in the lives of most people. They provide an opportunity for children and adults to learn the skills of caring, nurturing, and responsibility. People bring them into their homes, sometimes even making them a member of the family. So if you're family is a green family, how does your pet fit into the mix?

273 Think Again about that Exotic Animal

If you have your heart set on an exotic pet, there are some very important issues you need to think about. Some exotics are becoming more common and have been bred in captivity, like the ferret. But others, like parrots, are frequently captured in the wild. Methods used to catch and transport animals from the wild are harsh and often end up killing the animals. This is especially true with birds and reptiles. Some breeds are taken from the wild to the point of endangering the native population. Another consideration when looking at exotics is whether they are legal and how big and dangerous the animal may become as it grows. Even relatively small animals can pose dangers to humans, especially children.

274 Spay and Neuter

Spaying or neutering a pet is one of the greenest decisions you can make. There is an overpopulation of pets, both pure and mixed breed, and millions of animals are euthanized every year. Many programs are available to assist with the cost of neutering or spaying a pet. There are also programs to spay and neuter cats that have been abandoned or are strays. These feral cats are wary of people and congregate in groups for protection and food. By releasing them back to their environment, the cats are allowed to stay together without multiplying.

THE CHOICES YOU CAN MAKE . . . **WHEN CARING FOR YOUR PET**

275 Pick Out Pet Food and Treats

Owners love their pets and want to make sure they are feeding them well, but do you know what you're really feeding your pet? Pet food contains protein from various sources. The protein comes primarily from the ground remains of animal processing such as the heads, feet, and intestines; it is the discards of the human food industry. The meat processed into by-product meal or meat and bone meal may be from sick or healthy animals. The meat products are processed through an extruder that steams the material under high pressure to form food nuggets. This processing destroys the nutritional value, requiring manufacturers to add nutrients and minerals back into the product. Preservatives are also added to pet food to ensure that it lasts for months, in the grocery store and at home.

276 Assess What's Actually in Pet Food

When choosing a pet food, it's important to pick a brand that has an Association of American Feed Control Officials (AAFCO) guarantee and cites feeding tests or feeding profiles, not just nutrient profiles. Many natural recipes will include higher quality protein without by-products. Look for labels that include identified meat like chicken, lamb, or beef as the first ingredient, not just the word *meat*. Natural pet food will most likely not use chemical preservatives but will rely on vitamins C and E to partially or fully preserve food. As an added bonus, some natural foods are sold in recycled packaging. Note that if you want to change your pet's diet, it's important not try it all at once. A sudden change may upset an otherwise healthy pet's digestive system. A small portion of the new food can be mixed with a larger portion of the old food to slowly introduce more and more of the new food.

277 Make Homemade Pet Food

One sure way to know your pets are getting a balanced and natural diet is to make their food at home. This may also prove successful if your animal companion suffers from reactions from commercial food. If planning to make homemade pet food, it's important to meet the animal's nutritional requirements. You can consult a veterinarian or a veterinary nutritionist on the appropriate breakdown of protein, vegetables, and grain and any other vitamins or minerals that need to be added.

278 Buy Green Bedding and Other Gear

Green bedding can be made from organic cotton or hemp stuffed with recycled polyester. Toys made from organic and recycled materials are also on the market. Cat trees are now made from reclaimed untreated wood, giving cats real trees to perch on. Training agents can be environmentally friendly, too. Grannick's Bitter Apple manufactures products to keep dogs, cats, birds, ferrets, horses, and small animals from chewing on things they shouldn't—from your furniture to themselves. There are organic shampoos and skin treatments available that use organic, biodegradable ingredients. The popularity of the green movement along with the need to pamper pets has led to a market for organic grooming products.

279 Be Dutiful with Doggie Doo

Many cities have laws requiring dog owners to pick up after their pets when walking in someone else's yard or in a public place. The best solution in picking up an animal's droppings is to use a biodegradable bag. That way when it's disposed, the bag will degrade along with the droppings. You can find them at pet stores and at many gathering spots like doggie parks and campgrounds. Some cities, like San Francisco, are developing ways to make the most of dog feces by

converting it into methane that can be used for fuel. The city part-
nered with Norcal Waste Systems to collect waste from a dog park in
San Francisco for a pilot program in 2006. Norcal fed the feces into a
methane digester. Some dairy operations use similar digesters, feeding cow dung into the digester to convert it into methane to supply
electricity.

280 Take a Closer Look at that Litter

Even when cleaned regularly, litter boxes can smell and are usually
surrounded by litter that's been tossed about by kitty. Most kitty litters are made from clay that is mined, and any mining operations are
very hard on the earth. Regardless of the reclamation performed,
the land can never be returned to pristine conditions once the mining
is complete. Mining operations disrupt the land surface by removing all the trees and the topsoil, rerouting storm water onto and off
of the site. They generate waste, which can include the release of
metal contamination into the groundwater. The good news is that
alternatives for filling the cat box include biodegradable litter. Green
options include litter made from recycled paper or reclaimed wood.
Not only do these litters avoid mining operations, they utilize post-
consumer waste that would otherwise be sent to a landfill. If you are
planning to switch your kitty to biodegradable or recycled litter, you
may need to do it gradually, adding a little at a time so as not to con-
fuse the cat.

281 Consider Holistic Animal Health Care

Just as with human doctors, it's important to make sure you see eye-
to-eye with your veterinarian. Some pet owners are very happy with
traditional vets while others seek the extended services of a holistic
practitioner. Holistic vets have degrees in traditional veterinary medicine but take additional course work in more natural approaches to

THE CHOICES YOU CAN MAKE . . . **WHEN CARING FOR YOUR PET**

healing and helping animals. Holistic medicine is generally used to treat chronic conditions, not traumatic injuries.

282 Make Sense of Alternative Vet Care

Holistic vets also look at alternative medicines that can be applied to animals such as the following:

- Acupuncture
- Behavior modification
- Chiropractic therapy
- Herbal remedies
- Homeopathy
- Nutritional therapy

When it comes to other aspects of pet care such as flea control, owners should make sure they are on the same page as their vets in looking for solutions that everyone feels comfortable with.

283 Find Safe Options for Flea Control

A plethora of synthetic chemicals on the market can help owners wage war on fleas. These dips, sprays, and topical ointments all contain pesticides that are absorbed into a pet's body through their skin. Fleas are able to build up a resistance to these chemicals, requiring new formulas to be produced. While these flea treatments work very well in most cases, they can pose a danger to the pet and possibly even others in the house. Potential risks with using flea treatment can be researched on the EPA Web site (*www.epa.gov/pesticides/factsheets/flea-tick.htm*), which contains fact sheets for a variety of active ingredients.

284 Control Fleas with Soapy Water

You can set flea traps by placing a soapy dish of water under a light. The fleas will be attracted to the warmth and will drown in the soapy water. Also, when combing out pets, keep a cup of soapy water handy. Pull fleas off the comb and drop them into the water; the soap makes it difficult or impossible for the fleas to escape, leaving the tiny biters in a watery grave.

285 Don't Release Animals Back to the Wild

Animals that have been domesticated, even if they were born in the wild, may not fare well on their own. Domesticated animals exist in a world without predators and with a constant food supply. Putting them out on their own leaves them at risk. Without care, many released animals will likely starve, fall prey to predators, be hit by cars, or die from disease. Released animals that survive can wreak havoc on their new surroundings. The introduction of a new species upsets the local balance already in place between animals and the environment.

286 Consider These Scary Scenarios

In October 2005 wildlife officials in the Everglades National Park found a thirteen-foot long python that bit off more than he could handle when he tried to down a 6-foot alligator. The python's girth wasn't big enough and it literally busted at the seams. Neither the alligator nor the python survived. If a new home is needed for a pet companion, owners should work to find one. Vets and local rescue organizations can sometimes help find pets new homes.

CHAPTER 17
The choices you can make . . .
WHEN CELEBRATING A HOLIDAY

287 Have a Jolly Green Holiday

Holidays give people the chance to express gratitude, share company, eat well, and occasionally take time off from work or school. No matter what the holiday, it's likely to come with pressures to shop, decorate, give gifts, and feed friends and family. But before getting caught up in the holiday hype, take a step back and think about what the occasion really means—and how you can celebrate without doing too much damage to the planet.

288 Learn the History of the Holiday

The 1970s saw the advent of a new holiday that helped solidify the environmental movement. The annual planetary celebration was dubbed Earth Day. Gaylord Nelson, a Democratic senator from Wisconsin, started the holiday. Growing up in northwestern Wisconsin, Nelson enjoyed exploring the outdoors, and as a senator, one of his speaking points was the environment. Nelson strongly believed that the environment—and the impact people had on it—was not receiving the attention it deserved. He worked with President John F. Kennedy, who shared his belief, even doing a conservation tour in 1963. Still unable to get a foothold in the political movement, environmental concerns were perpetually relegated to the backseat as other pressing issues gained recognition.

289 Celebrate the Planet's Very Own Holiday

During the summer of 1969, Gaylord Nelson was speaking about conservation and witnessed the energy of antiwar demonstration's teach-ins. He knew then that if he could harness similar enthusiasm for the environment, his battle to protect the planet would be successful. He organized a day of observance for environmental issues—April 22, 1970. In preparing for the event, the media and other politicians clamored to be involved, helping to make it a day like no other and striking the match that would fuel the environmental movement. Today Earth Day is celebrated in a variety of ways, from community events and parades to political gatherings. Many use the day to promote environmental issues such as sustainable living and global climate change. The Earth Day Network (*www.earthday.net*) includes a list of celebrations and some ideas for organizing an event.

290 Consider Consumerism on a Deeper Level

The holiday season conjures up images of blinking lights, crowded shopping malls, and lots and lots of presents. The term usually refers to that stretch on the calendar between Thanksgiving and New Year's Day that includes a variety of different celebrations. It's a time of year that marks the viability of the economy. But are shopping and spending really such a good idea? The holidays bring families and friends together, but there is a lot of stress over excess spending, hectic schedules, and the potential to overindulge on just about everything. The holidays also generate a lot of waste. If you want to scale back, you don't need to change years of tradition, but a little cutting equals less environmental impact.

291 Simplify Your Experience

When looking at ways to simplify, consider starting with decorations. If your family purchases a Christmas tree, a living tree might be a good choice. Living trees can be purchased and planted after the holidays are over. Or if you buy an artificial tree, it can be used over and over again. If you don't have a place to plant a living tree but want the authenticity of a real tree, make sure to recycle your cut tree. When you put up ornaments, let the tree show. If some needles show after all the ornaments are hung, that's okay. Not every branch needs to be glittering and sparkly. If you need more ornaments, consider making them from recycled materials. There are tons of Web sites and library books with great ideas for ornaments, and if you remember to date your new ornaments you can look back and reminisce every year.

292 Dim Down the Place—a Lesson in Holiday Lights

When lighting up inside or out, lower-wattage lights can bring about the same glitter and gleam without the expense. Not only do smaller lights burn less electricity, they produce less heat, making them safer. Light-emitting diode (LED) holiday lights are new on the scene. They cost about $8 more than a standard strand but will last up to ten years and use less electricity. Remember to put your lights on a timer so they automatically shut off. Here's where a little procrastination can pay off. The later you wait to put them up, the less time they'll be using extra energy.

293 Plan a Creative Gift Exchange

When it comes to partying, consider swapping cookies instead of gifts. If you plan a cookie exchange, have guests share stories about their recipes. Was it a hand-me-down from a beloved aunt or a brand-new recipe from an easy cooking guide? Some hosts ask guests to bring a dozen cookies for each guest, but you can adjust the numbers as you like. Your flexibility and creativity as a host will foster a festive atmosphere for everyone.

294 Have an Orange, Black, and Green Halloween!

It's a scary time of year filled with costumes and candy. The costume market has exploded as children and grownups dress like their favorite movie and television characters. But before splurging on a costume that may only be worn once, consider what's in the closet. See if there is anything that can be modified and mixed up to be used as a costume. Leftover 1980s clothes or an old sport coat can be the beginning of a retro-theme costume. Overalls and a plaid shirt can be the basis for a farm or scarecrow costume. A common theme for teens is dead anything—from a dead prom queen to a dead baseball player. All it takes is an old dress or uniform and some scissors and makeup. If your closets aren't serving up any costume ideas, visit a local consignment shop.

295 Don't Go Overboard with Halloween Traditions

Scary jack-o'-lanterns yield a lot of waste. Don't throw your pumpkin's guts away after you're done carving. Use the meat to make muffins or a pie and the seeds are delicious baked and salted for snacks. When the jack-o'-lantern has seen his last day, toss him on the compost pile instead of throwing him to the curb. This may sound cheap, but don't go overboard giving out candy either. It's rare for kids to go home without candy spilling out of their buckets and bags. More candy given out means more candy bought, and the more candy bought means the more candy made and the more waste produced!

296 Send a Message of Hope with a Green Greeting Card

It's more of a tradition with winter holidays, but that doesn't stop stationers from promoting more and more special occasion cards. Forgo the Halloween and St. Patrick's Day cards altogether if you're seeking to be greener, or consider sending e-cards to friends and family. Also, holiday cards don't have to be thrown as away as soon the occasion passes. They can be made into a variety of useful items. Fronts can be reused to make new cards, bookmarks, gift tags, and lace-up toys. If sending cards or holiday letters just isn't a tradition you are willing to give up, consider sending only a letter. Use hand stamps to make it festive. Another alternative is to purchase cards from your favorite charity. Choose an organization that sends a message you support and uses recycled materials.

297 Being Green Doesn't Make You a Scrooge!

According to *42 Ways to Trim Your Holiday Wasteline*, written by Robert Lilienfield and Dr. William Rathje, the authors of the *ULS Report* (*www.use-less-stuff.com*), 25 percent more trash is tossed during the holiday and shopping season than at any other time of year. When it comes to season's greetings, 2.65 million holiday cards are sold each year. That's enough to fill a football stadium ten stories tall. It's not humbug to practice conservation and reduce your mailing list.

298 Make Your Gift Count

Gifts are integral to most holidays and special occasions, but take a minute to think before you purchase. Don't buy a token gift that will soon be forgotten just because you feel obligated. Think about what resources it took to make and package the gift and what will become of it after the special day. It's not that you should feel guilty when making a purchase, but it is worth considering where it came from, where it will go, and how it fits into the whole scheme of things.

299 Shop for Green Gifts

Consider buying friends and family canvas bags to take shopping or items made from recycled materials like street signs or old album covers. Chances are there won't be any awkward duplicates with unique recycled gifts. Also, gifts made with love can be particularly sweet. Knowing someone made homemade soap or jewelry really adds a personal touch to the holiday or occasion. And consider gifts of entertainment or endowment. Tickets to a stage show, sporting event, or a movie don't require excess packaging or wrapping. An evening out might be the perfect gift. Donations to a favorite charity are something to think about, too. A commemorative brick or the care and feeding of a sea bird may be a very special gift for someone who has everything.

300 Do a Good Deed

Instead of buying a gift for neighbors or relatives, do something nice. Rake their lawns, shovel their sidewalks, or take on another chore. This is particularly nice if they really don't want anything. Some people would rather not be given gifts that they must find a place for or figure out what to do with. This is the perfect opportunity to make frozen meals, put together an emergency kit, give a gift certificate for a nearby grocery store, or make a gift basket of essentials such as stamps, envelopes, and pens. Don't forget about photos; put them in a small book or on a magnet or mug.

301 Wrap in "Green Paper"

You've picked out the perfect gift. Now what? Consider a reusable bag or box to wrap the present. For paper options, try comics, maps, coloring pages, or wrapping made from recycled paper. Use scarves to secure a gift. The wrapping can even be part of the gift, using containers like flowerpots and dishes. For gift tags, cut up used greeting or holiday cards so the art on the card serves as the front of the gift tag and write a message on the back. If there is writing on the back, just glue a piece of paper with your message over it. When sending gifts, try to reuse shipping materials like padded envelopes, cartons, and peanuts, and think about how the gift will be sent when you're shopping for it. Smaller and lighter may be easier and greener to package and send. If the gift is staying local, avoid wrapping altogether. Hide the gift and send the recipient on a scavenger hunt to retrieve it.

302 Practice Smart Entertaining

Entertaining can vary from an extended visit from out-of-town friends and family to a fancy one-night shindig. If the evening requires entertaining a large group of people, turn the heat down before your guests arrive. Also depending on the theme, consider whether decorating is really necessary. If you do need some zing, make your decorations. Create banners from recycled newsprint. Homemade banners are much more personal than mass-produced ones, and large rolls of recycled newsprint can be used for the banner and then reused as drawing paper throughout the year. One way to make birthday party decorations more special is to make a photo collage of the birthday celebrant.

303 Conserve in the Kitchen

Don't overcook. Meals should be planned according to the guest list. Consider who will eat what and what portions are appropriate. Don't feel obligated to offer guests every potential appetizer or entrée under the sun. There's no need to overfeed guests either. Don't throw leftovers away. Send them home with guests, pack them into your own refrigerator or freezer, or donate them to a shelter. Turkey carcasses and ham bones make for great soup. If there is a whole pie or untouched leftover, donate it to a local food bank. If leftovers outlive their useful life in the fridge, add them to the compost bin. However, meat and processed foods are not good for a compost bin if it is not rat proof.

304 Use Your Dishes

It may be mean extra work for you, but think about hosting the event with reusable dishes instead of disposable dishes. If it's a particularly formal event, borrow or rent dishes rather than buy them. When washing up after the affair, fully load the dishwasher to get the most out of the hot water. Put out separate bins for recyclables and label them so guests know where to toss their glass, plastic, and aluminum.

CHAPTER 18

The choices you can make . . .

WHEN INVESTING IN THE FUTURE

305 Watch the Greening of Big Business

Many corporations are starting to see the green in being green. Whether out of social and environmental concern or to cut costs and increase profits, more and more companies are looking to improve the construction and operation of their facilities and businesses. It's up to you as a consumer to communicate to these environmentally minded companies that you approve of their actions by doing business with them.

306 See How Small Corporations Make Their Mark

Many smaller companies operate with the environment in mind. However, as large corporations build more efficient and environmentally friendly buildings, perhaps the process will become part of the mainstream and more businesses will be encouraged to follow suit. Sustainable development has the potential to streamline the design and construction processes and possibly lower the cost of green construction, making it more viable for other companies that might not have been able to afford it.

307 Support Companies Based on Government Grading

The Environmental Protection Agency (EPA) evaluates companies on their environmental performance using the National Environmental Performance Track, a program that was started in 2000 to recognize public and private institutions that go above and beyond the minimum environmental requirements. Interested parties apply for the program by implementing an independently prepared environmental management program. They must also maintain a record of compliance with environmental laws, commit to achieving quantifiable goals, and provide information to the community on their practices.

308 Hold Companies Accountable

Beyond recognition, organizations that are required by law to submit environmental reports may benefit from a reduction in reporting and inspection requirements. That is why the National Environmental Performance Track lends itself primarily to organizations that utilize or impact resources that require permitting from the EPA or other environmental regulatory agencies, such as water, wastewater, and solid waste. The EPA estimates that since its inception the program's members have made great strides, including the following:

- Reduced water use by 1.9 billion gallons
- Reduced solid waste generated by almost 600,000 tons
- Increased use of recycled materials by 20,000 tons
- Set aside more than 1,000 acres for land conservation

Companies involved in the program manufacture anything from pesticides to auto parts, and they are trying to run at least portions of their operations in a more environmentally conducive way.

309 Spend with Environmentally Friendly Companies

There are private organizations that rate companies, allowing consumers to decide which businesses operate in ways that are most important to them. Organizations such as IdealsWork, Inc. classify different companies according to how they perform environmentally and socially. The organization was started by two friends with a drive to make the world a better place by giving consumers useful information to make informed decisions with their purchases. The result is a database of companies that manufacture products and businesses that provide services. Businesses are divided by type of operation and are ranked based on research performed by the Investor Responsibility Research Center.

310 Plan for Your Future and the Earth's, Too

Planning for your financial future can take into account the future of the planet, too. Many investors today understand that earnings don't have to be made at the expense of the environment, social justice, or public health. To invest socially, look for companies with good employee relations, a record of community involvement, and accomplished environmental stewardship. You'll also want to consider company track records in maintaining environmental compliance, utilizing alternative energy sources, and handling labor relations. Companies can be evaluated by using some of the resources you will find here.

311 Make Money and Make a Difference

Diversifying is important in any portfolio, and this can still be accomplished when the goal is maintaining environmentally friendly investments. To put together a socially responsible collection of stocks and bonds, check out the information on the Social Investment Forum (*www.socialinvest.org*), the Progressive Investor (*www.sustainablebusiness.com*), and SRI World Group's Social Funds (*www.socialfunds.com*). Rather than evaluating companies alone, you can turn to a financial adviser. Many financial firms that include socially and environmentally responsible companies in their portfolios, such as Calvert Group Ltd, rely on data from sources like the EPA National Environmental Performance Track to select investment options.

312 Participate in Charities and Organizations

Many nonprofit and charity organizations work hard to improve the lives of people and animals and protect the environment. In a move toward a greener lifestyle, you may decide that this is something you want do, not just as a feel-good measure but to help someone or

support a cause. A first step is to decide what kind of charity you would like to support. Are you more interested in helping protect land and ecology, farm animals, or impoverished people? Or is there another cause that hits home for you?

313 Designate Your Funds for a Specific Cause

Charities can buy the supplies they need with money donated from individuals. Often, you can even designate how you would like your contributed funds to be distributed. For example, you can donate to Earth Share and specify that you'd like your money to go toward the Scenic America organization. As a rule of thumb, monetary contributions should never be made in cash, and you should be sure to keep records and receipts. You can also choose to support a nonprofit in honor of someone else—maybe as a holiday gift! Beyond the altruistic feeling, an added benefit from donating is writing it off on your taxes.

314 Volunteer and Make a Difference

Besides contributing money to charities, you can also volunteer your time. By giving time, you will be able work on projects and meet other people. Projects might include building a house or clearing an area of an invasive species. Volunteering can go beyond task work and include helping run the program, providing some expertise in a specific field, and even being on the board of directors. Many charities do not have staff on their payroll and rely heavily on volunteers to manage the organization. Supporting jobs include filing documents, answering phones, staffing an office, doing data entry, and other behind-the-scenes tasks. Time is a valuable commodity that many charities need and appreciate. Giving your time shows that you are concerned and helpful.

315   Learn Something New

When offering to volunteer for a charity, you will likely be asked what skills you have and when you are available. While volunteering may give you the opportunity to use your skills, it may also give you the chance to learn something new. If you are handy with woodworking or painting, volunteering with Habitat for Humanity could give you the opportunity to learn about wiring and electrical work. Volunteering with some charities may even offer the opportunity to travel to other parts of the country or even overseas.

316   Choose the Charity for You

There are a variety of organizations available to help you choose a charity or volunteer opportunity if you are looking to expand your boundaries:

Action Without Borders at *www.idealist.org* connects charities with those looking to volunteer all over the world.
SERVEnet at *www.servenet.org* is a program of Youth Service America (YSA), which provides volunteer opportunities for young people from five to twenty-five years old to help foster citizenship.
VolunteerMatch at *www.volunteermatch.org* allows volunteers to find opportunities nationally, locally, and even virtually.
Wilderness Volunteers at *www.wildernessvolunteers.org* brings together hardworking people who love the outdoors with opportunities in forests and parks all over the United States.

317   Make Sure the Charity Is Legitimate

Whether donating time or money, you will want to make sure you're supporting a worthy charity and one that meets your standards. So

THE CHOICES YOU CAN MAKE . . . **WHEN INVESTING IN THE FUTURE** before giving to any charity, do your homework. There is information available that can be used to determine how forthright a charity is, helping to make sure that your money is going to help legitimate causes. You can do a background check to see how much of the money collected actually goes to charitable deeds, not to administrative support or fundraising work. Beware—some fundraising companies are for profit and keep a large portion of what they collect for themselves.

318 Check Your Charity

There are a number of organizations that provide valuable information on charities, making donating a safer and more rewarding experience. Here is a list of some of those organizations:

Charity Navigator at *www.charitynavigator.com* rates charities on a scale of one to four stars. Organizations are rated on characteristics such as expenses, earnings, and efficiency.

BBB Wise Giving Alliance at *www.give.org* performs analyses of national charities to provide donors with information so they can make informed decisions.

GuideStar at *www.guidestar.org* maintains a database of information including IRS forms, employee information, and grant activity on charities that is searchable by donors at different membership levels.

JustGive at *www.justgive.org* allows donors to find charities that are important to them. You can give money on the Web site and set up accounts for others to donate to the same charity.

The **I Do Foundation** at *www.idofoundation.org* allows happy couples to set up charitable wedding registries and give charitable favors.

Sites like these give credibility to those charities that deserve it and improve the altruistic community as a whole. Knowing which organizations will use contributed money most wisely helps donors feel even better about giving.

CHAPTER 19

The choices you can make . . .

WHEN PLANNING YOUR LEGACY

319 Consider a Green Burial

More and more people are choosing environmental burials for themselves and their families. New approaches to green burial practices are expanding, and the rise is expected to continue as more people learn their options and make plans for the inevitable.

320 Make a Plan for your Family Members to Follow

Make sure your loved ones know how you feel about end-of-life issues such as organ and tissue donation and funeral arrangements. If a funeral or ceremony is going to be different from the norm, it's best to settle on plans well in advance. When making arrangements for a green funeral, be sure to consider laws governing embalming or transportation that may become an issue. Community clergy and other religious figures should be familiar with the practices and rites allowed. Funeral directors usually offer guidance and direction through the process, but they may not be aware of all of the alternatives. That's why it's even more important to have a plan.

321 Consider Organ, Tissue, and Whole-Body Donation

Donating organs so that others live is the ultimate in recycling and reuse. Donate Life America estimates that eighteen people die every day while waiting for a transplant. Organs that can be transplanted include kidneys, lungs, liver, heart, pancreas, and intestines. Skin and bone can also be donated, as can corneas. The United Network for Organ Sharing (UNOS) is a nonprofit company that works under contract with the Department of Health and maintains the database for those needing organs. You may also choose to donate your entire body for medical research or education. Whole-body donations are usually run by state governments and universities. You can find a database of whole-body donation programs at *www.med.ufl.edu/anatbd/usprograms.html*. Generally, health issues don't impact

THE CHOICES YOU CAN MAKE . . . **WHEN PLANNING YOUR LEGACY**

whether a person can donate his or her body. Organs that cannot be used for transplant may still be suitable for research.

322 Understand the Need for Embalming

Studies have shown that after a person dies the population of bacteria and pathogens increases greatly. If precautionary measures are not taken, the act of embalming can expose morticians to disease, and embalming fluid decreases the overall chance of transmitting infection from the body to the mortician. Besides protecting funeral and mortician workers, the main purpose of embalming a body is to preserve it long enough for survivors to mourn and pay respects.

323 The Embalming Process Explained

Embalming fluid is comprised of a variety of chemicals. Because solutions are patented, specific ingredients are confidential. Generally they include antibacterial compounds, preservatives, fragrances, dyes, solvents, and surfactants. Some in the industry advocate the use of alternative embalming fluids that are capable of disinfecting and preserving bodies while reducing the environmental impact and health concerns for workers. The University of Toledo in Ohio performed limited studies in the vicinity of cemeteries to determine if embalming fluids impacted soil and groundwater. Results indicated that contaminant levels were detected but at minor concentrations.

324 Learn Why Preserving the Dead Is so Important

The process of preserving includes pumping embalming fluid into an incision at the carotid artery and then allowing it to drain from an incision at the jugular vein. Blood and other fluids are then removed from the body cavity. Embalming fluid with a higher concentration of formaldehyde is then pumped into the organs to preserve them. Per the Environmental Protection Agency (EPA), the fluid-blood mixture requires proper

THE CHOICES YOU CAN MAKE . . . **WHEN PLANNING YOUR LEGACY**

disposal as an industrial wastewater. It must either be flushed down the drain or containerized and taken to a permitted wastewater treatment facility. Funeral homes can apply for an underground injection control permit that would allow them to discharge to their own septic systems.

325 Should You Choose a Coffin or Casket?

The environmental impacts of being buried in a coffin include the potential for metals, varnishes, sealers, and preservatives used on wood caskets to be released into the environment. Limited studies showed that arsenic was present in soil but not groundwater and was more than likely caused by older preservation methods or from wood preservatives that contained arsenic. Embalming fluid and wood preservatives no longer contain arsenic, but these changes are relatively new. Many arsenic-treated coffins holding arsenic-embalmed bodies have already been buried. Unlike arsenic, formaldehyde used for embalming today breaks down rather quickly. Arsenic, however, collects in the soil, slowly leaching into groundwater over time.

326 Thinking about Natural Preparation?

There is a "do it yourself" funeral movement in which survivors take care of their loved ones and bury them on private land. Some find that handling their loved ones after death allows the process to remain personal and loving. Bodies are washed and dressed by close friends and family. Caskets, sometimes homemade, are decorated. Friends and family gather at the house, communing and sharing stories.

327 Make Sure It's a Lawful Burial

While home preparation and burial may seem natural, families must make sure it's handled correctly. By law, the body does belong to the family; however, there are state statutes that must be followed. This means anyone caring for a body is considered the funeral director and must meet all the regulatory requirements a funeral director has to meet. The death certificate has to be completed, embalming or other forms of preservation such as dry ice or refrigeration have to be addressed, a burial permit must be obtained if required by the state, and permits may need to be obtained to move the body. There are a number of organizations that can provide assistance to help make sure all the applicable laws are considered. The Funeral Consumers Alliance (*www.funerals.org*) provides information not just on less costly burial alternatives but also on the rights and responsibilities of loved ones. The group can also suggest an advocate to help the survivors if there is confusion or misinformation regarding legalities.

328 To Cremate or Not to Cremate

Cremation is becoming more popular in the United States, with ashes either being buried or scattered in the sea or the mountains. The decision whether to be cremated may be personal, religious, or societal. A benefit of using cremation prior to a service is that the body need not be preserved and the service can be scheduled at a later time. Because of the destructive nature of cremation, a death certificate signed by a medical examiner is required before it can take place. Some states require a time limit between death and cremation. If the body is not refrigerated prior to cremation, it must be embalmed. This can be handled with a crematorium or through a funeral home.

329 Consider the Effect of Cremation on Our Earth

During cremation, a completely combustible coffin and the body are burned at a very high temperature. There are concerns with the air pollution released during cremation. The primary concern with crematorium emissions is mercury released from dental fillings. Crematoriums are required to use what is referred to as the best available technology (BAT) to treat emissions, which includes directing releases through an air scrubber prior to release from a chimney. There are not, however, set air standards for crematoriums to meet.

330 Choose an Environmentally Friendly Casket

The casket is one of the more expensive burial components. On the simple end, caskets of cardboard or untreated wood provide the necessity without the added expense of chemicals or materials of more opulent coffins. There are many designs available that take the environment into account. Most of the environmentally friendly caskets available today are manufactured in Europe; however, as green burials gain in popularity, there will likely be more designs available in the United States. Some cemeteries allow the burial of limited types of caskets, so consult your cemetery before you decide on a coffin that may be less mainstream.

331 Consider Alternative Caskets

There is the standard pine box that's been used for hundreds of years. They can be purchased through a funeral home or from manufacturers. In fact, there's a company called the Old Pine Box (*www.theoldpinebox.com*) that offers pine coffins and coffins made from other sustainable trees. Some coffins come with metal components, but they can be ordered with rope handles and nontoxic glue. There's also the option of a homemade casket. Casket plans or complete kits can be purchased from companies like the MHP Network (*www.mhp-casketkits.com*). Carpenters or artisans can also be contracted to build a custom casket. Also, recycled-paper or cardboard caskets are one of the greener burial options. These are generally used for cremation, but they can also be used for burial. Most come in plain brown, but others are more artistic. Ecopods (*www.ecopod.co.uk*), made in the United Kingdom, are 100 percent recycled paper. They have sleek artistic designs and come in a variety of colors.

332 Pick a Final Resting Place

Even if a loved one is cremated, you'll need to decide what to do with the remains. For decades, burial in a standard cemetery has been the norm, but alternative resting places have become a business in themselves. For those who are cremated, ashes can be spread almost anywhere—sprinkled at sea, scattered in the woods, even incorporated into an art piece. Before spreading ashes, consider whether you'll want to visit the gravesite and what might become of the property where the ashes were placed. Will loved ones feel upset if the open field where the ashes were spread later becomes a discount store?

333 Check into Preserves

Preservations are still in their infancy but are growing as alternatives to run-of-the mill manicured and landscaped cemeteries. Considered green cemeteries, preserves let nature take over, leaving many trees in place and planting others as memorials. Nature preserves require that the deceased not be embalmed and that only environmentally friendly caskets or shrouds be used. Caretakers can usually help interested parties find acceptable products and materials. Although embalmed bodies are generally not accepted for burial, exceptions may be made if the deceased was embalmed against their wishes. Graves are marked with simple stones or native plants and can be documented with a global positioning system. Pets can also be buried on the property. Trails and boardwalks offer pathways for visitors who are coming to see a grave, taking a relaxing walk, or enjoying a bird-watching expedition.

334 Choose Natural Burial Grounds Carefully

Green cemeteries are unregulated, so take care in choosing one. The Green Burial Council (*www.greenburialcouncil.org*) is working to begin certifying conservation burial grounds and natural burial grounds.

THE CHOICES YOU CAN MAKE . . . **WHEN PLANNING YOUR LEGACY**

A conservation burial ground offers a natural setting, provides for future conservation measures, and is located near parks, wildlife corridors, or permanently protected areas. A portion of the proceeds are set aside for perpetual care and the grounds are protected by a conservation easement, which means that legally the land cannot be developed. Natural burial grounds are similar, but they only provide protection of the burial ground, not the surrounding areas. Green burial locations, state laws, and more information can be found at *www.forestofmemories.org.*

335 If the Final Resting Place Is Under the Sea

It is possible to be buried at sea without being cremated. As part of the Clean Water Act, the EPA requires that burials at sea take place at least three miles offshore and where water is at least 600 feet deep. Remains must be in a container that will not float. If remains are cremated, they must still be taken three miles offshore, but there is no minimum water depth. Burial at sea has become its own industry, offering reef memorials and boating services. Eternal Reefs (*www.eternalreefs.com*) offers a concrete casting in which the remains are mixed with the concrete. Once the mixture is cast, family and friends can place their handprints or write messages on the outside of the form that will eventually rest on the ocean floor. The concrete forms can make an artificial reef and marine habitat.

336 Plan for Final Touches at Your Ceremony

There are alternatives to receiving flowers at the memorial service. Friends can be asked to donate native plants to a church, school, park, or center. Books that illustrate the deceased's environmental beliefs can be purchased for the local library. Money can be donated to an environmental charity in the name of the deceased. A scholarship can be set up for environmental studies to benefit a deserving student.

CHAPTER 20

The choices you can make . . .

WHEN YOU WANT TO DO MORE

337 Work for the Movement—Every Day

Working full-time, people put in about 2,000 hours a year at their jobs. With that amount of time, some people believe it is important to have a job that is rewarding to them and to the environment. The U.S. Department of Labor projects that the growth of careers in the environmental field, particularly hydrology and environmental engineering, will increase over the next decade and salaries will be competitive with other careers. More and more universities and colleges offer courses and degrees in environmental fields. There are many different green careers and educational paths—consider the possibilities!

338 Get into Green Fields of Study

The variety of jobs available in the environmental field range from those requiring bachelor's degrees and above to those that provide on-the-job training. Environmental careers can involve highly technical desk jobs or active work out in the field. When looking for a job, consider what you want to do and how you want to spend your time. Do you want to interact with the public or to be outside? Is designing environmental systems for landfills, water treatment plants, or even manufacturing facilities more up your alley? The field is awash with job opportunities—so much so that deciding on a career could be more difficult than landing a job.

339 Plan for Your Future

Choosing a major goes hand in hand with choosing a career. Some professions can be achieved with a variety of degrees, but others require very specific degrees and training. For example, conservation specialists may have degrees in biology or environmental science. But on the other hand, an engineer needs to have a degree in engineering. Also, some degrees provide stepping-stones to other careers. A person with an engineering degree can work as a regulator, and that may lead to a career in politics down the road. Not everyone entering a university knows exactly what career path he or she will follow, but students can analyze their interests, passions, and talents to decide on a career path.

340 Get in the Green Mindset When Picking a University

Choosing a university to attend should be based on the area of study. When considering a university or college, look at all the programs the school offers and what kind of jobs graduates find. If you plan on earning a master's or doctorate, take into account how well the undergraduate program has prepared past graduates. Make sure the program is accredited; this may directly impact your job opportunities, advanced degrees, and any certification or licensure you need. The Environmental Education Directory at *www.enviroeducation.com* has a searchable database for numerous fields of environmental study. The database includes a list of learning institutions from colleges and universities to more specialized centers such as the Audubon Expedition Institute run through Lesley University. If you are interested in graduate school, *www.gradschools.com* for lists of programs and universities leading to advanced degrees in environmental fields.

341 Look at the School's Master Plan

Universities and colleges rely on master plans that identify different operations—including transportation, waste generation and handling, and heating and cooling—and specify how they will be implemented. By incorporating environmental stewardship in preparing a master plan, these schools set examples and provide hands-on experience for students to take with them after they graduate. Master plans may incorporate sustainable considerations as the university ages and expands, constructing new buildings and refurbishing older ones. When building facilities, does the school administration encourage energy-efficient design? Is the equipment used by the administration, faculty, staff, and students energy-efficient?

342 Evaluate Energy Use on Campus

You may want to find out how waste is handled at the universities that interest you and if recycling programs are in place. Many schools of higher learning maintain their own incinerators, particularly if biomedical wastes are generated. If this is the case, ask if the university operates the incinerator as a cogeneration plan, providing electricity or hot water for the campus, and if the air emissions meet required standards. Another aspect you may want to consider is transportation. Many campuses provide shuttle services from off-campus locations. Switching to hybrid or biodiesel can increase the benefits of these shuttle services. Also, universities purchase many cars to be used by faculty and staff. When buying cars, does the university consider energy efficiency?

343 Consider Semi-Environmental Professions

While some occupations are inherently environmental, other careers—such as engineering, science, writing, public administration, and law—can have an environmental facet. Some jobs, like park rangers or camp counselors, allow workers to spend time outside and possibly educate others in learning about the environment, while other positions require most of the work to be done in the office with little interaction with nature.

344 Explore What the Job Will Entail

A big part of deciding what career path to follow is what the job will entail. From day to day work to lifetime commitments, if you want to be part of the environmental industry, you should do a bit of homework. Some careers take years of schooling and experience while others are easier to transition into—whether you are graduating from college and looking for your first job or, after years of working in another career, you decide to switch your focus to the environmental industry, there are numerous environmental professions out there. Ask yourself, can you be any of the following things . . .

345 Environmental Engineers

. . . design and permit all different types of environmental operations, including water treatment plants, wastewater treatment plants, solid waste facilities, and water and wastewater collection and distribution systems. Engineers can also design remediation systems to clean contaminated soil and groundwater. Engineers can work for federal, state, or local regulators overseeing operations in their district. They can also work in the private sector for consulting firms whose clients include cities and counties with environmental projects and operations.

346 Environmental Journalists

. . . research and write on environmental topics. They can work for nonprofit groups or media outlets as media consultants or correspondents. It is their responsibility as environmental journalists to be objective and present facts, not simply to promote propaganda or someone else's agenda. This requires an understanding of the topic, and the journalist must interview various professionals with different perspectives.

347 Geologists and Hydrologists

. . . work for industries and regulatory agencies and independently as consultants. They use their knowledge of the subsurface to evaluate

groundwater quality and availability. In areas where groundwater is the primary source of drinking water, geologists and hydrologists determine impacts from over-pumping and look to alternative supplies. In industry, they often work with mining and oil corporations. When groundwater has been contaminated, geologists and hydrologists assess the degree and extent of contamination.

348 Ecologists

. . . often advise groups that want to construct projects of potential environmental effects of the development. They survey areas, determining what species of flora and fauna exist and what impacts a project would have on the populations. They can work to eliminate negative impacts and suggest alternate approaches or supplemental work to enhance a project.

349 Toxicologists

. . . work to protect the public from environmental impacts. Circumstances arise where chemicals are released, exposing the public. A toxicologist evaluates the impact of those releases. Often, this is performed through a risk assessment through which the toxicologist calculates the possibility that a given contaminant at a given concentration will cause a disease. Toxicologists often work in the chemical and pharmaceutical industries and for regulatory agencies.

350 Conservation Scientists

. . . work to protect natural resources like soil, rangeland, and water. They develop plans and make recommendations to allow use of the natural resources with the least amount of environmental impact. With respect to soil, a conservation scientist might recommend ways to reduce erosion. With water, the scientist evaluates how to protect quality while providing drinking water to the public.

351 Foresters

. . . usually work with private timber companies or landowners, making sure that regulations are met when wood is harvested. They also encourage the healthy growth of forests and make recommendations when alternative operations or equipment should be considered.

352 Environmental Lawyers

. . . work for regulators, private industry, and activist organizations to interpret the meaning and applicability of environmental laws. It is not uncommon to see environmental lawyers on either side of a dispute, representing clients charged with polluting the environment and regulators that want the situation corrected. In working with activist organizations, lawyers often press the government to enhance enforcement actions or pass stricter legislation.

353 Urban and Regional Planners

. . . work to balance the needs of a community. They must take into account growth and expanded infrastructure, such as water and wastewater facilities. Most planners work for local government agencies and are required to attend public meetings.

354 Wildlife Biologists

. . . study how animals live in human-made or natural environments. Their roles may be similar to or overlap with ecologists. Wildlife biologists can be employed to determine what animals exist in a certain area and how changes may impact their populations. This is of importance in areas where endangered or threatened species exist.

355 Solid Waste Managers

. . . work for cities and counties and handle issues with garbage collection and disposal. They usually work with outside consultants to

THE CHOICES YOU CAN MAKE . . . **WHEN YOU WANT TO DO MORE**

help design transfer stations, landfills, and incinerators while making sure regulations are met. Solid waste managers educate the public in matters of disposal practices and recycling and can be key players in determining economical ways to recycle and discourage waste.

356 Wastewater Treatment Plant Operators

. . . run facilities that treat sewage. Sewage is processed through a plant where waste is collected and removed. The end result is treated water and sludge, a mud-like material that requires proper disposal. Properly run wastewater treatment plants abide by federal and state regulations. Treated water is often discharged to bays or rivers, while sludge is taken to a landfill or—depending on contaminant concentrations—used as fertilizer for farming operations.

357 Park Rangers

. . . operate parks, ensuring that the environment and wildlife are in good condition, and they also work to educate the public. They maintain facilities and make sure they are safe for animals as well as the people who visit. Some rangers with wildlife rehabilitation facilities provide a place for rehabilitating and releasing injured animals. The Internet offers a variety of Web sites that provide information on different environmental careers and job openings. Check out Green Dream Jobs at *www.sustainablebusiness.com* or the Environmental Career Center at *www.environmentalcareer.com*.

358 The EPA and Other Organizations

The Environmental Protection Agency (EPA) employs scientists, engineers, policy analysts, and lawyers. Not only does this agency help to enact and enforce environmental laws, it performs research and prepares policy. The EPA is responsible for protecting human health and the environment by supporting laws and defending and maintaining the quality of the air, water, and land. There are many organizations that work to save the environment. For example, the U.S. Fish and Wildlife Service monitors and enforces illegal trade, habitat destruction, and environmental contamination of wildlife habitats.

359 Work for the Government

The U.S. Department of State heads the Office of Environmental Policy, which works on a global level to institute policy geared toward worldwide impacts on air quality, toxic chemicals and pesticides, hazardous waste, conversion of critical habitat, and invasive species. This multilateral department works with organizations such as the United Nations and World Bank to develop policies that will protect the environment and afford sustainability for all cultures. Other departments and agencies that dabble in the environment include the U.S. Department of Energy and the Office of Energy Efficiency and Renewable Energy (*www.eere.energy.gov*). These offices administer alternative energy programs and provide information to consumers and businesses on solar, biomass, and other renewable options. There may be opportunities at the state level too, make sure to check with your local town-hall for more information.

360 Environmental Research

The federal government employs environmental researchers in many areas. These workers do not enforce environmental laws or regulations but work to collect, analyze, and maintain data for regulators and the public, as well as invent greener chemicals and materials. There are a variety of organizations and agencies within the government that perform research used to promote and protect the environment. The U.S. Centers for Disease Control and Prevention (CDC) also work to protect the public from environmental impacts. The CDC address health concerns regarding air and water quality as

THE CHOICES YOU CAN MAKE . . . **WHEN YOU WANT TO DO MORE**

well as exposure to toxic chemicals. You may also want to consider the National Center for Environmental Health (NCEH). The NCEH is a program within the CDC that works to eliminate illness, disease, and death from environmental impacts. And then there's the National Oceanic and Atmospheric Administration (NOAA). The NOAA carries out research to better understand the oceans and coasts and promote ecosystem-based management of natural resources.

361 Green Jobs *Really* Are Everywhere

Even the U.S. Department of Transportation, an agency that may not spring to mind when considering environmental opportunities, operates the Federal Highway Administration (FHWA), which works in part to encourage non-motorized means of transportation. The FHWA is currently working on a non-motorized transportation pilot program in four communities: Columbia, Missouri; Marin County, California; Minneapolis-St. Paul, Minnesota; and Sheboygan County, Wisconsin. The program aims to encourage biking and walking by building sidewalks and bicycle paths to and from highly trafficked areas such as transit stations, workplaces, schools, residential areas, and community centers. The information gathered during the program will be used to provide state and local agencies with means to increase non-motorized transportation.

362 Day-to-Day Work for a Nonprofit

There are non-governmental organizations that work to address environmental issues, largely when they feel that the government is not doing enough or that their hands are tied. Although their relationships with governmental agencies may some times be adversarial, nonprofits also provide important information to the government to direct policy. Earth Share, for example, is an umbrella network that includes leading environmental and conservation groups across the United States. Charity Navigator (*www.charitynavigator.org*) awarded Earth Share four stars, the highest rating for a charitable organization. Not all charities that fall under the auspices of Earth Share have received four-star ratings, so do background work on the ones that interest you.

363 Consider These Earth Share Charities

Here are a few of the charities that are included under the Earth Share umbrella:

Natural Resources Defense Council utilizes skilled lawyers and scientists to promote activism and evaluate political policies and legislation.

Clean Water Fund investigates and reports on water quality issues. A report prepared by the group in 2006 titled *Are We Still Wading in Waste?* documented how wastewater treatment plants report spills into waterways.

Union of Concerned Scientists works to protect the environment and public health by promoting the use of valid and accurate science.

Nature Conservancy uses a planned methodology to select important environmental properties and works with landowners to purchase them for protection. The organization also provides funds for areas to be studied to determine the environmental impact from different operations.

Rainforest Alliance works with companies, cooperatives, and landowners to protect ecosystems and the people and animals that depend on them.

There are vast numbers of nonprofits out there. Some nonprofits offer unpaid internships that enable students to receive college credit and gain valuable experience.

364 Get Involved—It's Easy

Many communities offer programs for their citizens to learn about different aspects of services provided in their area. You can take courses in ecology, energy efficiency, and waste management at your local community college. Or you can take tours of solid waste facilities, water and wastewater treatment plants, and even power substations. Participating in these programs will enlighten you about how your city or town operates. Local parks, outfitters, environmental groups, and community colleges also offer environmental courses and programs. These can range from exploring the different ecosystems in the area, such as tidal communities, to hiking through a nature preserve to observe the wildlife in local hardwood forests.

365 Spread the Knowledge

If you have experience in promoting the environment, you can use it to teach others. Share your knowledge and passion with others and introduce them to topics they may not have known about. If you operate a manufacturing facility that incorporates recycling, give a tour and let the public know. Not only will it educate the public on the importance of recycling, it can serve as an advertisement, too. If you are a skilled outdoors person, give a lecture or lead an expedition. It doesn't have to be complicated or dangerous, just down-to-earth and educational.